nibbled

200 fabulous finger food ideas

Published by Murdoch Books Pty Limited.

Murdoch Books Australia
Pier 8/9, 23 Hickson Road, Millers Point NSW 2000
Phone: +61 (0)2 8220 2000 Fax: +61 (0)2 8220 2558

Murdoch Books UK Limited
Erico House, 6th Floor North, 93–99 Upper Richmond Road
Putney, London SW15 2TG
Phone: + 44 (0) 20 8785 5995 Fax: + 44 (0) 20 8785 5985

Chief Executive: Juliet Rogers
Publisher: Kay Scarlett
Concept and art direction: Marylouise Brammer
Project manager: Grace Cheetham
Photographer: Tim Robinson
Stylist: Sarah DeNardi
Stylist's assistant: Loren Trompp
Home economist: Joanne Glynn
Recipes by: The Murdoch Books Test Kitchen
Recipe introductions by: Francesca Newby
Text editor: Rachel Carter
Designer: Annette Fitzgerald
Editorial director: Diana Hill
Production: Monika Vidovic

National Library of Australia Cataloguing-in-Publication Data
Nibbled. Includes index. ISBN 1 74045 450 2. 1. Appetizers. 2. Snack foods. 614.812

Printed by Midas Printing (ASIA) Ltd. Printed in CHINA.

IMPORTANT: Those who might be at risk from the effects of salmonella poisoning (the elderly, pregnant women, young children and those suffering from immune deficiency diseases) should consult their doctor with any concerns about eating raw eggs.

The publisher and stylist would like to thank the following companies for generously loaning furniture, fabric and tableware for photography: Mondo Luce, Smeg, Mud, Tres Fabu, Mandalay Designs, Waterford Wedgwood, Orrefors Kosta Boda, Georg Jensen, Radford Furnishings, Dinosaur Designs, Judy Porter Vintage, Cloth, Aero Plus and beclau. Special thanks go to the following companies: Signature Prints (Florence Broadhurst fabrics and wallpapers), Mokum Textiles (Osborne & Little fabrics and wallpapers), 'font & medley' for handmade placemats, Paper Couture for the gorgeous drinks invitation, Design Mode International (iittala tableware), 'dwell by jo' for the Flip-Flop sofa; Marble Works and aeria Country Floors for tiles; Chee Son & Fitzgerald, Glory Designs, Spence & Lyda and Ken Neald C20th Modern for fabulous fabrics, lamps and furniture; Iris and Hazel for models clothing. Finally, a heartfelt thanks to our patient model/assistant Loren and assistants Brielle and Cara.

nibbled

200 fabulous finger food ideas

Photography by Tim Robinson
Styling by Sarah DeNardi

MURDOCH BOOKS

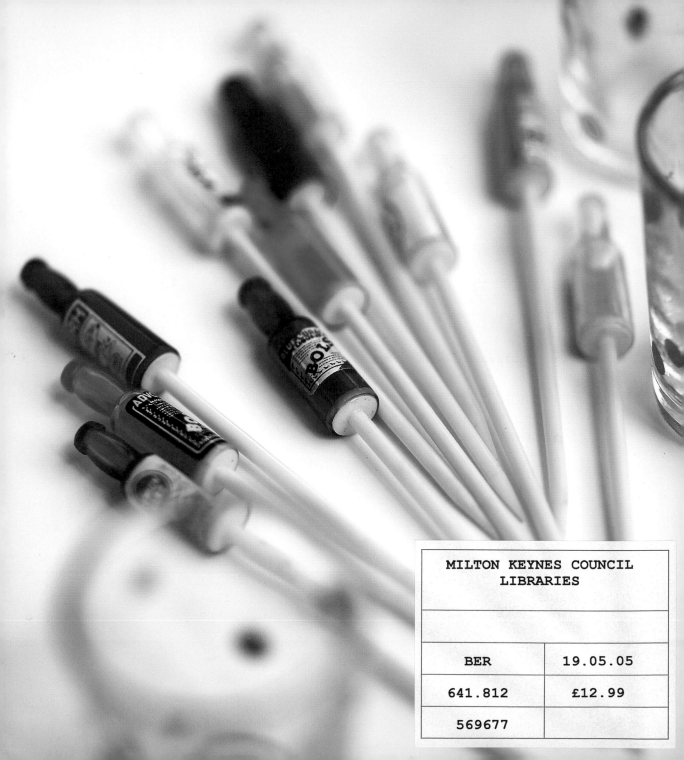

contents

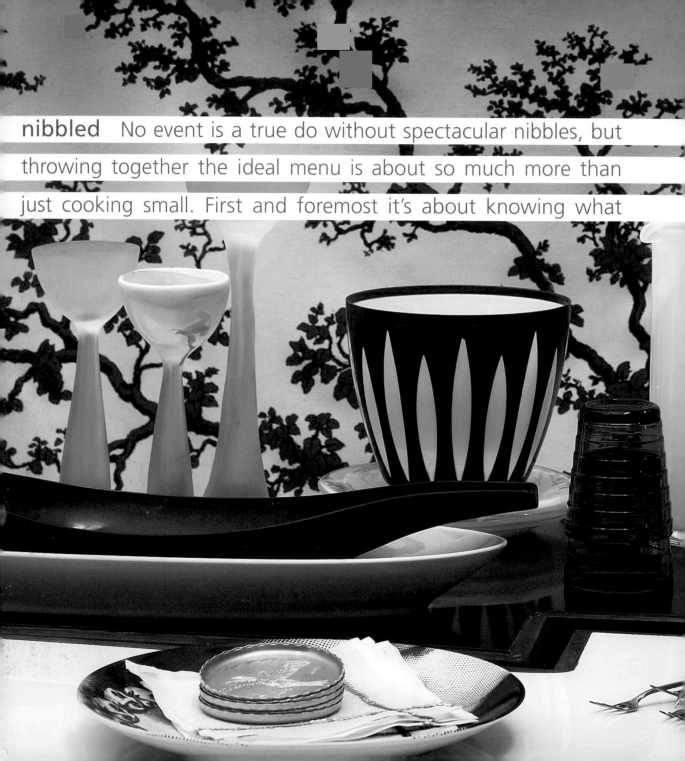

nibbled   No event is a true do without spectacular nibbles, but throwing together the ideal menu is about so much more than just cooking small. First and foremost it's about knowing what

kind of party you want — from a sophisticated tea party to a glam evening of cocktails. Just add a little bit of planning and a good dash of inspiration for a fabulous occasion.

nibbled

The key elements to take into account when planning a menu of nibbles are the type of event you are catering for, the tastes of your guests and number of people you are expecting. To help with this we've divided this book into five chapters designed to reflect the five most common types of party at which you'd expect to serve nibbles: brunch, outdoor lunch, tea, cocktails and lounge. Each of these events is defined by both the time of day it is held and the kind of ambience you want to create.

Regular party goers fall into two key categories — those who see the food as the main event, and those who simply view it as a way to help the drinks go down. With a little bit of imagination, it's easy to plan a menu that caters for both of these groups and creates a cohesive mood. Whatever type of party you're holding, from breakfast through to a midnight feast, the cardinal rule is to make sure that there is enough food for everyone. Hungry guests can easily turn into beyond-tipsy guests. So don't even think about under-catering; plan to be super generous and then ramp up the quantities by another third. With this in mind, it's time to start planning an event that will live on in the memory of all those who are lucky enough to be invited.

The tastes, likes and dislikes of your guests should play an important role in your menu selection. If you're having a small party with close friends this shouldn't be hard to achieve, but if you are throwing a large bash or catering for someone else, you will need to include some variations. Vegetarian options are a must and you may also want to dish up some dairy-free and wheat-free nibbles as well as low-carb delicacies.

Numbers have a significant impact on the style and tone of any party and they'll certainly have an impact on the menu you select. The two main considerations are the amount of work required to prepare the food and any issues of presentation involved. It goes without saying that the more fiddly a dish is to prepare the harder it will be to make it in bulk. Not that this should be a reason to discount a delicacy that appeals to you — it simply requires a greater depth of planning. If you're hosting a major event with hordes of people, don't even consider trying to do it all yourself. The trick here is organization and delegation. Make sure you are clear on what kind of help you need and which tasks need to be completed in which order. Stock up on soft drinks, chips and dips for any willing helpers and get the party started in the kitchen.

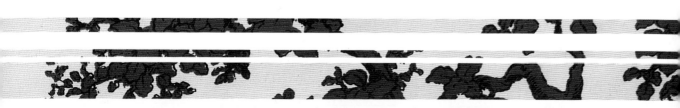

While it can definitely be easier to cater for smaller numbers, different considerations come into play. At a crowded party it's fine to be dashing in and out of the kitchen, doing a little mingling, handing round a platter and generally flitting about. With a small gathering, though, the name of the game is intimacy and conversation, an atmosphere that is hard to create if you're squirreled away in the kitchen. Keeping this in mind, it's wise to create a menu that allows you to prepare as much as possible beforehand so that you are able to be both present and relaxed when guests arrive.

Although it is the quality and flavour of the food that your guests will appreciate the most, the way in which it is served can add glamour and verve to the simplest event. White platters are the standard fallback for serving nibbles for a good reason — they offer a neutral background that allows the food to stand out and are an easy way to create a simple and cohesive style. If, however, you are confident about experimenting with the food you serve, why not throw caution to the wind and experiment with the way in which you present it? Creating a look for your party is another tool in the quest to create atmosphere.

If you're catering for a crowd, put together a flotilla of hostess trolleys for a cute and easy way to serve mountains of food. Tea looks oh so pretty served on mismatched plates from delicate old dinner services. Head to your closest charity shop and put together a whole new look on a shoestring. If the food leans towards Asia, stock up on mini bamboo steamers as a cheap and funky way to dress up the food. And lastly, don't forget to turn to the outdoors for beautiful ways to dress up the food — flowers, twigs, leaves and stones all lend an uncontrived beauty to a plate of fabulous food.

Food, drinks, music, company and atmosphere are all important elements of any successful party. The most vital element, though, is you. While fabulous food will make your party memorable, the guests have come to see you and you'll miss all the fun if you're chained to the stove. If you're at all nervous about your catering abilities, start small and keep it simple. Stick to recipes you know or, if you must experiment, have a practice run first. If impact is essential, pull out all the stops, but don't try to do it on your own. The best way to ensure that a good time is had by all is to mix, mingle and flirt to the best of your ability.

champagne brunch   Pop open some bubbly, pile platters with goodies and start the weekend with a bang. Breakfast celebrations are a charming choice for a get-together. We're usually at our best mid-morning, so start at a civilized hour and get the party rolling.

Sweets are always a winner, so are savouries — bubbly and brioche, scallops and salsa, fried eggs and fritters; mix up an eclectic feast.

Brunch has a rhythm all of its own. Some will have eaten already, others will wait, but either way you're free to indulge in some wilder flavours and combinations. The lunch element is what makes brunch so special: the combination of brekky treats and lunchtime delights allows for twice the grazing pleasure in one meal. It's important to assume that your guests might not have eaten yet. Empty stomachs demand special consideration in several different ways. Many of us are a little squeamish when it comes to the first meal of the day; make sure you offer a good selection of comfort food for those who find it hard to look a coffee in the face first thing. Serving drinks at an early hour can be a heady way to start the day so make sure you offer enough food to go around or things may get a little sticky. Going for an early rather than later party also gives you less time to prepare so figure this into your schedule when planning the menu. Brunch also allows you to experiment with drinks. Try toe-curlingly good bellinis, bucks fizz or kir royales, and whip up frothy, luscious smoothies for those who choose not to imbibe. Neither event would be complete without excellent-quality coffee and tea. If you don't have a coffee machine, now is the time to beg, borrow or steal one. Recruit a willing volunteer to man the machine and complement the delicious food with steaming hot drinks.

tomato and basil bruschetta

1 large loaf Italian (ciabatta)
    bread or French bread stick
2 tablespoons extra virgin olive
    oil, plus extra for brushing

4 ripe tomatoes, finely chopped
1 large handful basil, finely
    shredded

Cut the bread into 1 cm (1/2 inch) slices, then brush with olive oil and cook under a hot grill (broiler) until golden on both sides.

Mix together the tomato, basil and olive oil and season well. Spread the mixture over the toast and serve immediately.

Makes about 30

smoked salmon and caper bruschetta

2 small French bread sticks
250 g (9 oz/1 cup) cream cheese
2 tablespoons lemon juice
3 tablespoons chopped chives

small slices of smoked salmon,
to garnish
baby capers, rinsed and drained,
to garnish
dill sprigs, to garnish

Cut the bread sticks into 1 cm ($^1/_2$ inch) slices and cook under a hot grill (broiler) until golden on both sides.

Mix the cream cheese with the lemon juice and chives. Spread the mixture over the toast and top with small slices of smoked salmon and a few baby capers. Garnish with the dill sprigs before serving.

Makes about 24

The earthy aroma of mushroom perfumes these dainty frittatas garnished with an elegant shaving of Parmesan.

mini mushroom frittatas

25 g (1 oz) butter
8 small Swiss brown mushrooms, cut into quarters
80 g (2¾ oz) very small button mushrooms
2 eggs
3 tablespoons cream
1 tablespoon plain (all-purpose) flour
1 tablespoon finely chopped chives
2 tablespoons finely chopped parsley
2 tablespoons grated Parmesan cheese
6 pieces shaved Parmesan cheese, to serve

Heat the butter in a small frying pan over medium heat. When sizzling, add the mushrooms and cook for 5 minutes. Remove and allow to cool.

Preheat the oven to 180°C (350°F/Gas 4) and generously grease six holes in a muffin tray.

In a bowl, combine the eggs, cream, flour, chives, parsley and Parmesan. Season well with salt and pepper. Stir in the mushrooms and spoon the mixture into the muffin holes. Bake for 15 minutes. Cool for 5 minutes before removing from the tray. Serve warm, garnished with a piece of shaved Parmesan.

Makes 6

mini mushroom frittatas

quail eggs with spiced salts

2 teaspoons cumin seeds
48 quail eggs
125 g (4^1/$_2$ oz/^{1}/$_2$ cup) good-
   quality table salt

1^1/$_2$ teaspoons five-spice powder
3 teaspoons celery salt

Toast the cumin seeds in a dry frying pan over low heat for 1–2 minutes, or until richly fragrant. Cool slightly, then grind to a fine powder.

Put half the eggs in a large saucepan of water, bring to the boil and cook for 1^1/$_2$ minutes for medium- to hard-boiled eggs. Remove from the pan and rinse under cold water to cool. Repeat with the remaining eggs.

Divide the table salt among three small bowls. Add the five-spice powder to one, the celery salt to another and the ground cumin to the third. Mix the flavourings into the salt.

To serve, pile the eggs into a large bowl and serve with the three bowls of spiced salts. Invite your guests to peel their own eggs, then dip them into the flavoured salt of their choice.

Makes 48

petit croque-monsieur

16 slices white bread
125 g (4¹/₂ oz/¹/₂ cup)
   wholegrain mustard
100 g (3¹/₂ oz) thinly shaved
   honey ham
100 g (3¹/₂ oz) thinly sliced
   Jarlsberg cheese

55 g (2 oz/¹/₃ cup) very finely
   chopped mustard fruits
   (optional)
40 g (1¹/₂ oz) butter
2 tablespoons olive oil

Spread each slice of bread with mustard. Lay out eight bread slices on a board, mustard-side-up, and top with the shaved ham, then the cheese slices. If you are using mustard fruits, sprinkle them over the cheese. Press the remaining bread slices on top, mustard-side-down, to make eight sandwiches. Trim off the crusts, then cut each sandwich into three fingers.

Melt half the butter and oil in a non-stick frying pan. When the butter begins to foam, cook half the fingers until crisp and golden on both sides and the cheese is just starting to melt. Remove and keep warm on a baking tray in the oven. Melt the remaining butter and oil in the frying pan and cook the remaining fingers. Serve warm.

Makes 24

Elegant pearls of salmon roe glisten enticingly on top of these delicate blini, bringing a fresh and appetizing burst of colour.

buckwheat blini with smoked salmon

7 g sachet dried yeast
pinch of sugar
250 ml (9 fl oz/1 cup) warm milk
100 g (3^1/$_2$ oz/^{3}/$_4$ cup) buckwheat flour
60 g (2^1/$_4$ oz/^{1}/$_2$ cup) plain (all-purpose) flour
2 eggs, separated
20 g (^{3}/$_4$ oz) butter
4 tablespoons oil
150 g (5^1/$_2$ oz) crème fraîche
300 g (10^1/$_2$ oz) smoked salmon, cut into 2 cm (^{3}/$_4$ inch) strips
50 g (1^3/$_4$ oz) salmon roe
dill sprigs, to garnish

Put the yeast and sugar in a small bowl and gradually stir in the milk. Sift the flours into a large bowl and make a well in the centre. Add the egg yolks and warm milk mixture and whisk until combined and smooth.

Cover and leave the dough in a warm place for 45 minutes to prove.

Melt the butter, stir into the proved dough, and season. Put the egg whites in a clean dry bowl and beat with electric beaters until soft peaks form. Fold one-third of the egg whites into the batter. Gently fold in the remaining egg whites until just combined.

Heat 1 tablespoon of the oil in a large frying pan over medium heat. Drop $1/2$ tablespoon of batter into the pan for each blini. Cook for 1 minute, or until bubbles form on the surface. Turn over and cook for 30 seconds, or until golden. Repeat with the remaining batter to make about 40 blini, adding more oil when needed. Cool completely.

Spread 1 teaspoon of crème fraîche on each blini, then arrange a strip of smoked salmon over it. Spoon $1/4$ teaspoon of salmon roe on top. Garnish with a sprig of dill and serve.

Makes about 40

quail eggs with spiced salts

petit croque-monsieur

tartlet pastry cases

250 g (9 oz/2 cups) plain
    (all-purpose) flour
125 g (4^1/$_2$ oz) chilled
    butter, chopped
1 egg

Preheat the oven to 200°C (400°F/Gas 6). Lightly grease 30 mini muffin holes. Sift the flour into a large bowl and rub the butter in with your fingertips until the mixture resembles fine breadcrumbs. Make a well in the centre, add the egg and mix with a flat-bladed knife, using a cutting action until it comes together in beads. If the dough seems too dry, add a little cold water. Press the dough into a ball on a lightly floured surface, then wrap it in plastic wrap and refrigerate for 30 minutes.

Roll out the chilled dough between two sheets of baking paper to 2 mm (^{1}/$_{16}$ inch) thick and cut out 30 rounds with a 6 cm (2^1/$_2$ inch) cutter. Press a round into each muffin hole. Prick the bases with a fork and bake for 6–8 minutes, or until dry and golden. If they puff up, use a clean tea towel to press out any air pockets. Cool before filling.

Makes 30

tartlets with creamed egg and roe

4 eggs and 4 egg yolks
80 g (2³/4 oz) unsalted butter
4 tablespoons roe
30 cooked tartlet cases
    (see facing page)

Lightly beat the eggs and egg yolks together. Melt the butter in a small saucepan over very low heat, then add the eggs and whisk slowly and constantly for 5–6 minutes, or until the mixture is thick and creamy but the eggs are not scrambled. Remove from the heat straight away and season to taste with salt and cracked black pepper.

Fill each cooled pastry case with 1 teaspoon of the creamed egg mixture, top with ¹/2 teaspoon of roe and serve.

Makes 30

Ideally suited to breakfast, polenta muffins make a warm and
tasty base for the sublime mix of prawns and dill mayonnaise.

mini polenta muffins with prawns and dill mayonnaise

250 g (9 oz/2 cups) plain (all-purpose) flour, sifted
110 g (3³/4 oz/³/4 cup) polenta
1 tablespoon baking powder
55 g (2 oz/¹/4 cup) sugar
2 eggs, lightly beaten
125 g (4¹/2 oz) butter, melted
250 ml (9 fl oz/1 cup) milk
3 tablespoons finely chopped dill
1 tablespoon lemon juice
1 teaspoon horseradish cream
375 g (13 oz/1¹/2 cups) whole-egg mayonnaise
30 small cooked prawns (shrimp)

Preheat the oven to 200°C (400°F/Gas 6) and lightly grease 30 mini muffin holes. Sift the flour into a large bowl, add the polenta, baking powder, sugar and $^1/_2$ teaspoon of salt and mix together well. Add the egg, butter and milk and stir until just combined. Spoon small amounts into the muffin holes, filling to the top. Cook for 15–20 minutes, or until lightly browned. Turn onto a cake rack to cool.

Mix together the dill, lemon juice, horseradish cream and mayonnaise, and season with plenty of salt and black pepper.

When the muffins are cool, cut a circle from the top, as you would with a butterfly cake, and spoon a little dill mayonnaise on the muffin. Top with a prawn and some freshly ground black pepper.

Makes 30

mini polenta muffins with prawns and dill mayonnaise

corn and potato fritters

2 large potatoes
265 g (9^1/$_2$ oz/1^1/$_3$ cups) tinned
   corn kernels, drained
4 eggs, lightly beaten
6 spring onions (scallions),
   chopped
50 g (1^3/$_4$ oz/^{1}/$_2$ cup) dry
   breadcrumbs

1 teaspoon garam masala
3 tablespoons oil

dipping sauce
160 g (5^3/$_4$ oz/^{2}/$_3$ cup) plain
   yoghurt
2 tablespoons chopped mint
2 teaspoons sweet chilli sauce

Peel and coarsely grate the potatoes. Drain on paper towels and squeeze out the excess moisture. Combine in a bowl with the corn, eggs, spring onion, breadcrumbs and garam masala. Mix well.

To make the dipping sauce, combine all the ingredients in a bowl.

Heat 2 tablespoons of the oil in a heavy-based frying pan over medium heat. Cook heaped tablespoons of the mixture for 2 minutes on each side, or until golden. Drain on crumpled paper towels and keep warm. Repeat until all the mixture is used, adding extra oil to the frying pan if necessary. Serve with the dipping sauce.

Makes about 40

herb pancakes with avocado butter

60 g (2¼ oz/½ cup) plain
   (all-purpose) flour
60 g (2¼ oz/½ cup)
   self-raising flour
1 egg, lightly beaten
125 ml (4½ fl oz/½ cup) milk
4 tablespoons fresh mixed herbs
1 teaspoon cracked black pepper
melted butter, for pan frying

2 tablespoons baby capers, fried

avocado butter
½ ripe avocado, mashed
60 g (2¼ oz) butter, softened
1 tablespoon lemon or lime
   juice
½ teaspoon cracked black
   pepper

Sift the flours into a large bowl and make a well in the centre. Gradually add the combined egg, milk, herbs and pepper, whisking until the batter is smooth and free of lumps.

Heat a frying pan and brush with melted butter. Drop teaspoons of batter into the pan and cook until bubbles appear on top. Turn and cook until golden underneath. Keep warm.

To make the avocado butter, mix the ingredients together until smooth. Spread on top of the pancakes, garnish with the baby capers and serve.

Makes about 50

Savoury spinach mingles temptingly with the herby centres of the quail eggs to create a morsel with substance and style.

mini eggs florentine

8 slices white bread
olive oil, for brushing
12 quail eggs
2 teaspoons lemon juice
85 g (3 oz) butter, melted and cooled
2 teaspoons finely chopped basil
20 g (3/4 oz) butter, extra
45 g (1 1/2 oz/1 cup) baby English spinach leaves

Preheat the oven to 180°C (350°F/Gas 4). Cut 24 rounds from the bread with a 4 cm (1 1/2 inch) cutter. Brush both sides of the rounds with oil and bake for 10–15 minutes, or until golden brown.

Add the quail eggs to a small saucepan of cold water, bring to the boil, stirring gently (to centre the yolk) then reduce the heat and simmer for 4 minutes. Drain, then soak in cold water until cool. Peel, then cut in half. Remove the yolks and reserve the whites.

Put the egg yolks and lemon juice in a food processor and blend for 10 seconds. With the motor running, add the melted butter in a thin stream. Add the basil and process until combined.

Melt the extra butter in a saucepan, add the spinach leaves and toss until just wilted. Put a little spinach on each bread round, top with half a quail egg white and fill the cavity with the egg and basil mixture.

Makes 24

herb pancakes with avocado butter

smoked salmon and rocket rolls

185 g (6^1/$_2$ oz/^{3}/$_4$ cup) ricotta
    cheese
60 g (2^1/$_4$ oz/^{1}/$_4$ cup) crème
    fraîche or sour cream
2 teaspoons wasabi paste
1 tablespoon lime juice
12 slices brown bread, crusts
    removed

300 g (10^1/$_2$ oz) smoked salmon
100 g (3^1/$_2$ oz/1 small bunch)
    baby rocket (arugula),
    trimmed
baby rocket (arugula) leaves,
    extra, to garnish

Mix together the ricotta, crème fraîche, wasabi and lime juice.

Roll the bread out with a rolling pin to flatten.

Spread the ricotta mixture on the bread slices, then top with the smoked salmon and rocket leaves, leaving a border. Roll up firmly, wrap tightly in plastic wrap to hold the shape, then refrigerate for 30 minutes.

Unwrap, trim the ends and cut into 2 cm (^{3}/$_4$ inch) slices. Garnish with the extra rocket leaves.

Makes 36

citrus saucy scallops

24 scallops on the half shell
3 tablespoons lime juice
1 tablespoon lemon juice
1 small red chilli, seeded and
    finely chopped

1 tablespoon fish sauce
2 teaspoons sugar
3 teaspoons chopped coriander
    (cilantro) leaves
2 teaspoons chopped mint

Preheat the oven to 180°C (350°F/Gas 4). Using a sharp knife, carefully cut the scallops from their shells, as cleanly as possible, and remove the vein and white muscle. Wash the shells in hot water and warm through on a baking tray in the oven for 5 minutes.

Cook the scallops in a chargrill pan (griddle) or frying pan over high heat for 1–2 minutes each side, then return to their shells.

Combine the lime juice, lemon juice, chilli, fish sauce, sugar, coriander and mint. Spoon 1 teaspoon over each scallop and serve.

Makes 24

The flavour of goat's cheese is intensified during cooking, lifting the comfortable egginess of tortilla into the sublime.

potato, goat's cheese and herb tortilla

1 tablespoon olive oil
2 small potatoes, peeled and diced
1 small red onion, finely chopped
75 g (2^1/$_2$ oz) goat's cheese, crumbled
6 eggs
1 tablespoon chopped parsley
^{1}/$_2$ teaspoon thyme leaves

Heat the oil in a 19 cm (7^1/$_2$ inch) ovenproof frying pan over low–medium heat and cook the potatoes for 10 minutes, turning often. Add the onion and continue to cook, turning often, for a further 10 minutes. Remove from the heat and sprinkle on the goat's cheese.

Preheat the grill (broiler) to medium. Combine the eggs in a bowl with the parsley and thyme and season well. Return the frying pan to medium heat and gently pour the egg mixture over the potatoes. Cook for 3–4 minutes, or until the sides begin to puff up (gently lift the tortilla with a spatula occasionally to check that it is not burning).

Cook under the grill for 4–5 minutes, or until set on top. Cool, then slide onto a chopping board and cut into small wedges. Serve warm.

Makes 8–10 pieces

potato, goat's cheese and herb tortilla

scallop ceviche

16 scallops on the half shell
1 teaspoon finely grated
   lime zest
2 garlic cloves, chopped
2 small red chillies, seeded
   and chopped

3 tablespoons lime juice
1 tablespoon chopped parsley
1 tablespoon olive oil
2 small red chillies, extra,
   seeded and shredded

Preheat the oven to 180°C (350°F/Gas 4). Using a sharp knife, carefully cut the scallops from their shells, as cleanly as possible, and remove the vein and white muscle. Wash the shells in hot water and warm through on a baking tray in the oven for 5 minutes.

In a bowl, mix together the lime zest, garlic, chilli, lime juice, parsley and olive oil and season with salt and freshly ground black pepper. Add the scallops to the dressing and stir to coat evenly. Cover with plastic wrap and marinate in the refrigerator for 2 hours to 'cook' the scallop meat.

To serve, slide each of the scallops back onto a half shell, spoon on the dressing and scatter the shredded chilli on top.

Makes 16

bloody mary oyster shots

4 tablespoons vodka
125 ml (4 fl oz/1/2 cup)
    tomato juice
1 tablespoon lemon juice
dash of Worcestershire sauce
2 drops of Tabasco sauce

pinch of celery salt
12 freshly shucked oysters
1 cucumber, peeled, seeded
    and cut into julienne strips

Combine the vodka, tomato juice, lemon juice, Worcestershire sauce, Tabasco and celery salt in a jug. Mix well, then refrigerate for 30 minutes, or until chilled.

Fill 12 shot glasses about two-thirds full of the vodka mixture. Drop an oyster in each glass, then top with a teaspoon of julienned cucumber. For the final touch, crack some black pepper over the top of each shot glass, then serve.

Makes 12

Omelette rolls are divine when loaded with sour cream and caviar, and the egg on egg imparts a symmetry of taste.

rolled omelette with ocean trout caviar

4 eggs
4 tablespoons thick (double/heavy) cream
4 tablespoons finely chopped chives
1 tablespoon olive oil
40 g (1^1/$_2$ oz) butter, melted
3 slices white bread
3 tablespoons sour cream
100 g (3^1/$_2$ oz) ocean trout caviar or salmon roe
chopped chives, extra, to garnish

In a bowl, whisk together 1 egg, 1 tablespoon of cream and 1 tablespoon of chives and season with salt and pepper. Pour into a 25 cm (10 inch) lightly greased non-stick frying pan and cook over medium heat on one side for 3 minutes, or until just set (the omelettes will be difficult to roll if they are cooked for too long). Turn out onto a sheet of baking paper. Repeat with the remaining eggs, cream and chives to make four omelettes.

Tightly roll one omelette into a neat roll, then take another omelette and wrap it around the first. Repeat with the remaining omelettes so that you have two rolls. Wrap them separately in plastic wrap and refrigerate for 1 hour.

Meanwhile, preheat the oven to 180°C (350°F/Gas 4). Put the oil and butter in a bowl and mix them together. Using a 3 cm (1 1/4 inch) cutter, cut 24 rounds from the bread and brush with the butter and oil mixture. Arrange the rounds on a baking tray and bake for 20–30 minutes, or until crisp and golden. Remove and leave to cool.

Cut each of the cooled omelette rolls into 12 rounds. Spread 1/2 teaspoon of sour cream onto each croûton, and sit an omelette round on top. Put a teaspoon of salmon roe on top and garnish with a sprinkling of chives.

Makes 24

scallop ceviche

smoked salmon and avocado salsa

200 g (7 oz) smoked salmon,
    cut into thin strips
4 spring onions (scallions),
    finely chopped
2 1/2 large handfuls parsley,
    finely chopped

1 tablespoon baby capers,
    rinsed and drained
1 large avocado, diced
1 teaspoon grated lime zest
3 tablespoons lime juice

Combine the salmon, spring onion, parsley and capers in a bowl, then cover and chill in the refrigerator until ready to serve.

Just prior to serving, gently fold the avocado and combined lime zest and juice into the salsa. Delicious served with bruschetta.

Serves 4–6

mussels with bloody mary sauce

24 black mussels
2¹/₂ tablespoons lemon juice
salt, for spreading
2 tablespoons vodka
2 tablespoons tomato juice
1 tablespoon lemon juice

2 teaspoons Worcestershire
 sauce
dash of Tabasco sauce
¹/₄ teaspoon celery salt

Scrub the mussels and remove the beards (discard any that are open and don't close when tapped). Put the mussels in a large heavy-based saucepan with the lemon juice and 1 tablespoon of water. Cover and steam over medium–low heat for 2–3 minutes, removing them as they open. Discard any mussels that haven't opened in that time.

Remove the top shell, then run a small knife under the mussel to detach it from the shell. Arrange the mussels in their shells on a baking tray that has been spread with a layer of salt (this will keep them level and stop the filling falling out).

Combine the vodka, tomato juice, lemon juice, Worcestershire sauce, Tabasco and celery salt. Spoon 1 teaspoon into each shell and cook under a hot grill (broiler) for a few seconds, or until the sauce is warm. Serve sprinkled with freshly ground black pepper.

Makes 24

Slightly spicy and not too sweet, these babies are dangerously addictive little morsels and a sunny way to start the day.

baby banana breads with passionfruit butter

350 g (12 oz/1¹/2 cups) caster (superfine) sugar
2 eggs
125 ml (4 fl oz/¹/2 cup) vegetable oil
2 ripe bananas, mashed
215 g (7¹/2 oz/1³/4 cups) plain (all-purpose) flour
¹/2 teaspoon baking powder
¹/2 teaspoon ground cinnamon

passionfruit butter
250 g (9 oz/1 cup) spreadable cream cheese
3 tablespoons icing (confectioners') sugar
3 tablespoons passionfruit pulp, including the juice
2 teaspoons lemon juice

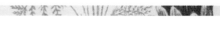

Preheat the oven to 180°C (350°F/Gas 4) and generously grease twelve 8 x 3 cm (3^1/4 x 1^1/4 inch) mini loaf tins.

In a large bowl, whisk together the sugar and eggs. Add the oil and 2 tablespoons of warm water. Whisk for 1 minute, then stir in the banana.

Sift the flour, baking powder and cinnamon into the bowl and stir to combine. Spoon the mixture into the tins and bake for 15–18 minutes, or until a skewer inserted into the centre comes out clean.

To make the passionfruit butter, combine the cream cheese and icing sugar in a food processor. Transfer to a bowl and stir in the passionfruit pulp. Add the lemon juice, a little at a time, to taste. Serve with the baby banana breads.

Makes 12

baby banana breads with passionfruit butter

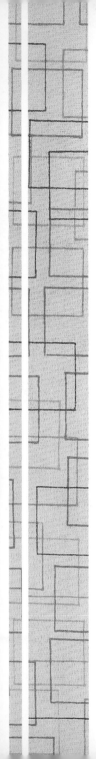

chocolate strawberries

250 g (9 oz/1 punnet) large
   strawberries
150 g (5½ oz) good-quality
   dark chocolate

100 g (3½ oz) good-quality
   white chocolate

Remove the leaves from the strawberries and brush with a dry pastry brush to remove any dirt. Line a baking tray with baking paper.

Melt the dark chocolate in a small heatproof bowl over a saucepan of simmering water, making sure the bowl does not touch the water. Dip the bottom half of each strawberry in the chocolate, then transfer to the baking tray and leave to set.

When set, melt the white chocolate in a small heatproof bowl over a saucepan of simmering water, then dip the tips of the strawberries in the chocolate. Return to the baking tray and allow to set.

Makes about 12

fruit bites with warm chocolate sauce

fresh fruit, chopped into
    24 pieces
250 g (9 oz) good-quality
    dark chocolate

185 ml (6 fl oz/$^3/_4$ cup) cream
1 tablespoon golden syrup
2 tablespoons chocolate- or
    orange-flavoured liqueur

Thread three pieces of fruit onto eight small skewers.

Combine the chocolate, cream, golden syrup and liqueur in a small heatproof bowl. Put the bowl over a saucepan of simmering water, making sure the bowl does not touch the water, and stir until melted. Serve with the fruit skewers.

Makes 8

These sweet fritters dusted in spicy cinnamon are a positively melt-in-the-mouth experience, bursting with juicy grapes.

grape fritters with cinnamon sugar

cinnamon sugar
2 tablespoons caster (superfine) sugar
1 teaspoon ground cinnamon

2 eggs, separated
1/2 teaspoon vanilla essence
3 tablespoons caster (superfine) sugar
150 g (51/2 oz) seedless red or black grapes
40 g (11/2 oz/1/3 cup) self-raising flour
40 g (11/2 oz) unsalted butter

To make the cinnamon sugar, combine the sugar and cinnamon in a bowl.

Whisk the egg yolks with the vanilla and sugar until combined and just creamy. Cut each grape into four slices, then stir the grape slices into the egg yolk mixture. Sift in the flour.

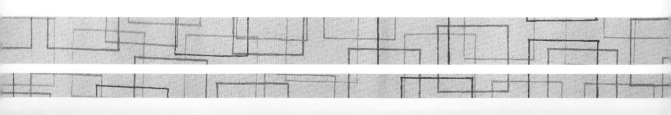

Beat the egg whites in a clean bowl until soft peaks form. Using a metal spoon, lightly fold half the egg whites into the egg yolk mixture until just combined, then repeat with the rest of the egg whites.

Melt 2 teaspoons of butter in a frying pan over low heat. Put 6 heaped teaspoons of batter in the pan to make six fritters and cook for 2–3 minutes, turning very carefully when the base becomes firm and bubbles appear around the edges. Flip gently and cook for a further 1–2 minutes, or until golden. Remove to a plate and keep warm. Repeat three times to make 24 fritters. Dust the warm fritters with cinnamon sugar and serve warm.

Makes 24

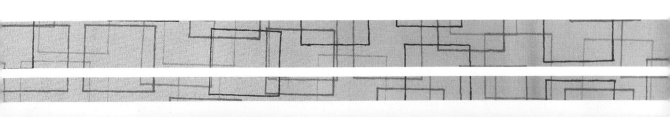

fruit bites with warm chocolate sauce

grape fritters with cinnamon sugar

custard and fruit tarts

4 sheets ready-rolled sweet
   shortcrust pastry
1 vanilla pod
315 ml (11 fl oz/1¼ cups)
   milk
2 egg yolks
2 tablespoons sugar

3 tablespoons plain (all-purpose)
   flour
375 g (13 oz) mixed fruit (such
   as strawberries, blueberries,
   kiwifruit), cut into pieces
3 tablespoons apricot jam,
   warmed and sieved

Preheat the oven to 180°C (350°F/ Gas 4). Lightly grease 24 baby tart tins. Cut the pastry into 24 rectangles to fit the tart tins. Put the pastry in the tins and prick the bases several times with a fork. Bake for 12–15 minutes, or until golden brown. Remove and leave to cool.

Cut the vanilla pod in half and put in a saucepan with the milk. Slowly bring to the boil, then remove from the heat and cool slightly.

In a large heatproof bowl, whisk the egg yolks and sugar until thick and pale. Add the flour. Remove the vanilla pod from the milk, then gradually whisk the milk into the egg mixture. Return to a clean pan over medium heat and stir constantly for 5–10 minutes, or until the custard boils and thickens. Allow to cool, then spoon evenly into each pastry case and top with the fruit slices. Glaze with the warm apricot jam.

Makes 24

petits pithiviers

almond filling
45 g (1¹/₂ oz) butter
40 g (1¹/₂ oz/¹/₃ cup) icing
   (confectioners') sugar
1 egg yolk
70 g (2¹/₂ oz/²/₃ cup) ground
   almonds

1 teaspoon finely grated orange
   zest
few drops of almond essence

3 sheets ready-rolled puff pastry
1 egg, lightly beaten

To make the almond filling, beat the butter and icing sugar with electric beaters until light and creamy. Add the egg yolk and beat well. Stir in the ground almonds, orange zest and almond essence.

Lightly grease two baking trays. Lay the puff pastry on a work surface and cut into 48 rounds with a 5 cm (2 inch) cutter. Divide the almond filling among half the rounds, using about 1¹/₂ teaspoons of filling for each, and leaving a 5 mm (¹/₄ inch) border. Brush the border with beaten egg. Put the remaining pastry rounds over the filling and press the edges firmly to seal. Transfer to the baking trays and refrigerate for about 30 minutes. Preheat the oven to 210°C (415°F/Gas 6–7).

With a blunt-edged knife, gently press up the pastry edges at intervals. Carefully score the pastry tops into wedges, then brush with beaten egg. Bake for 10 minutes, or until lightly golden.

Makes 24

Bite-sized pavlovas oozing cream and bursting with colourful fruit are an irresistible way to brighten up brunch.

mini pavlovas

3 egg whites
125 g (4^1/$_2$ oz/1 cup) icing (confectioners') sugar
150 g (5^1/$_2$ oz) good-quality dark chocolate, melted
250 ml (9 fl oz/1 cup) thick (double/heavy) cream
1 tablespoon icing (confectioners') sugar, extra
1 teaspoon finely grated orange zest
assorted fresh fruit (such as strawberries, cut into thin wedges,
    sliced pawpaw and kiwifruit) and passionfruit pulp, to garnish

Preheat the oven to 150°C (300°F/Gas 2). Put the egg whites in a large bowl and beat until stiff peaks form. Set the bowl over a large saucepan of simmering water and add the icing sugar to the egg whites while continuing to beat. Add it carefully or it will fly all over the place. At this stage it is best to use electric beaters as you must now beat the meringue until thick and very solid.

Using a cutter as a guide, draw 4 cm (1 1/2 inch) circles onto two sheets of baking paper, then invert these sheets onto baking trays (so the pencil won't come off on the pavlovas). Spread a little of the meringue mixture over each round — this will be the base of the pavlova. Spoon the remaining meringue into a piping bag fitted with a 5 mm (1/4 inch) plain piping nozzle. Pipe three small circles on top of each other on the outer edge of each base, leaving a small hole in the centre. Bake for 30 minutes, or until firm to the touch. Cool in the oven with the door slightly ajar.

When cold, dip the bases of the meringues into the melted chocolate to come about 2 mm (1/16 inch) up the sides of the meringues, then transfer to trays lined with baking paper and leave to set.

Combine the cream, extra icing sugar and orange zest until just thick. If necessary, beat slightly. Spoon into a piping bag fitted with a small plain nozzle and pipe into the meringues. Top with fruit and passionfruit pulp.

Makes about 40

custard and fruit tarts

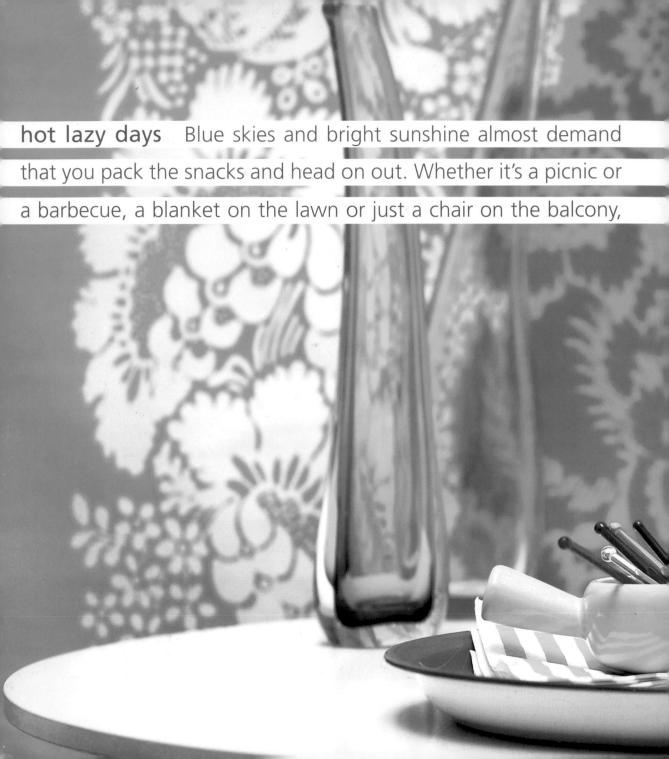

hot lazy days Blue skies and bright sunshine almost demand that you pack the snacks and head on out. Whether it's a picnic or a barbecue, a blanket on the lawn or just a chair on the balcony, outdoor food calls for a relaxed and languid vibe with unfussy food and minimal work in the field. A hamper and a corkscrew are the essentials to soak up the flavours of summertime.

Nibbles have the wonderful quality of being incredibly adaptable. It's so easy to throw together a menu that will satisfy the most diverse range of palates. When planning an outdoor lunch think of the menu as being like a tasting plate or a degustation menu — instead of offering your guests one large option, you can tantalize them with a carefully thought-out range of complementary flavours. Portability is a major consideration when planning a successful picnic. Presentation is always a priority but here the key is getting the food from A to B intact and at the right temperature. This isn't too hard if you're staying close to home and kicking back in the garden, but a trip further afield requires a little forward planning and a few extra tricks. Styrofoam boxes are plain but they will keep the food warm or cold for a good few hours. Or you could try tracking down some Indian tiffin trays, an excellent way of transporting hot food that looks fab too. Hampers work like they're meant to and always look pretty. Think of the outdoors as another room and put a bit of effort into dressing it up. Rugs and cushions make for comfortable lounging. Pretty napkins, plates and glasses all add to the effect. And garden torches can be lit when the afternoon heads for evening. If you want to go all out, fabrics draped in a tree can achieve a lovely effect. Then all you need is a bat, a ball, some delicious wines and fruit juices and a bunch of friends for a gorgeous afternoon in the sun.

salmon and tuna skewers

600 g (1 lb 5 oz) salmon fillet
500 g (1 lb 2 oz) fresh tuna
oil, for brushing
2 tablespoons lime or lemon juice

Soak 20 small wooden skewers in water for 1 hour. Cut the salmon and tuna into 2 cm (3/4 inch) cubes and season well with salt and pepper. Thread alternately onto the skewers, using three pieces of fish on each.

Heat a barbecue hot plate or chargrill pan (griddle) to hot and brush lightly with oil. Cook the skewers for 3–4 minutes, turning frequently and basting with a little lime or lemon juice as they cook.

Makes about 20

beef with black bean sauce skewers

1 kg (2 lb 4 oz) rump steak
30 bay leaves
4 tablespoons black bean sauce
oil, for brushing

Cut the steak into 2 cm (^{3}/4 inch) cubes and make small slits in the meat with a sharp knife. Trim the leaves off the bay leaf stems and thread the meat onto the stems. Brush lightly with the black bean sauce.

Heat a barbecue hot plate or chargrill pan (griddle) to hot and brush lightly with oil. Cook the skewers for 2–3 minutes on each side, brushing with any remaining black bean sauce during cooking.

Makes 30

Satay sticks are fabulous for picnics, barbecues or any outdoor meal — pack the spicy sauce and cook the skewers on the spot.

satay chicken skewers

12 chicken tenderloins, trimmed
    and halved lengthways
1 garlic clove, crushed
3 teaspoons fish sauce
2 teaspoons grated fresh ginger
lime quarters, to serve

satay sauce
2 teaspoons peanut oil
4 red Asian shallots, finely chopped
2 garlic cloves, chopped
2 teaspoons grated fresh ginger
2 small red chillies, seeded and finely chopped
200 ml (7 fl oz) coconut milk
125 g (4^1/$_2$ oz/^{1}/$_2$ cup) crunchy peanut butter
2 tablespoons grated palm sugar or soft brown sugar

2 tablespoons lime juice
1¹/₂ tablespoons fish sauce
2 teaspoons soy sauce
1 makrut (kaffir lime) leaf

Soak 24 wooden skewers in water for 1 hour. Combine the chicken, garlic, fish sauce and ginger. Cover, then refrigerate for 1 hour.

To make the satay sauce, heat the oil in a saucepan over medium heat. Add the shallots, garlic, ginger and chilli and cook for 5 minutes, or until golden. Add the rest of the ingredients, then reduce the heat and simmer for 10 minutes, or until thick.

Thread each chicken strip onto a skewer, then cook on a hot barbecue hotplate or chargrill pan (griddle) for 3–4 minutes, turning during cooking. Serve with satay sauce and lime wedges.

Makes 24

satay chicken skewers

hummus

220 g (8 oz) dried chickpeas

4 tablespoons olive oil

3–4 tablespoons lemon juice

2 garlic cloves, crushed

2 tablespoons tahini

1 tablespoon ground cumin

Soak the chickpeas in water for 8 hours or overnight. Drain. Transfer to a saucepan, cover with cold water, then bring to the boil and boil for 50–60 minutes, or until tender. Drain, reserving 185–250 ml (6–9 fl oz/ 3/4–1 cup) of the cooking liquid.

Put the chickpeas, oil, lemon juice, garlic, tahini, cumin and 1/2 teaspoon of salt in a food processor and blend until the mixture begins to look thick and creamy. With the motor running, gradually add the reserved cooking liquid until the mixture reaches the desired consistency.

Makes 550 g (1 lb 4 oz/2 1/2 cups)

herb and garlic pitta chips

100 g (3$^{1}/_{2}$ oz) butter
4 garlic cloves, crushed
1 tablespoon chopped thyme

2 teaspoons chopped marjoram
2 teaspoons chopped rosemary
2 pitta breads, split in half

Preheat the oven to 180°C (350°F/Gas 4). Mix together the butter, garlic, thyme, marjoram and rosemary. Spread the mixture over the pitta rounds and cut each piece into six to eight triangles. Bake for 5–10 minutes, or until crisp and golden. Store for 1 day in an airtight container and, if necessary, crisp up in the oven for a few minutes.

Makes about 30

These party pies with an exotic twist are a tempting treat at a grown-up gathering for the young at heart.

moroccan lamb mini pies

filling
2 tablespoons olive oil
1 onion, thinly sliced
2 garlic cloves, crushed
2 teaspoons ground cumin
2 teaspoons ground ginger
2 teaspoons paprika
1 teaspoon ground turmeric
1 teaspoon ground cinnamon
500 g (1 lb 2 oz) lamb fillet, diced
375 ml (13 fl oz/1 1/2 cups) beef stock

1 tablespoon finely chopped preserved lemon peel
2 tablespoons pitted Kalamata olives, sliced
1 tablespoon chopped coriander (cilantro) leaves

750 g (1 lb 10 oz) ready-rolled shortcrust pastry
1 egg, lightly beaten

To make the filling, heat the oil in a large saucepan over medium heat, then add the onion, garlic and spices. Coat the lamb in the spice mixture, then pour in the stock. Cover and cook over low heat for 30 minutes. Add the preserved lemon and cook, uncovered, for a further 20 minutes, or until the liquid has reduced and the lamb is tender. Stir in the olives and coriander, then leave to cool.

Preheat the oven to 180°C (350°F/Gas 4) and put a baking tray in the oven. Grease twelve 5 cm (2 inch) shallow tart holes.

Roll the pastry thinly and cut out 12 rounds with an 8 cm (3^1/4 inch) cutter. Using a 5.5 cm (2^1/4 inch) cutter, cut out 12 smaller rounds from the remaining pastry. Put one of the larger rounds in each tart hole and fill with the cooled filling. Dampen the edges of the small rounds and put them on top of the filling to seal the pies. Trim the edges and brush with egg. Put the tin on the hot baking tray and bake for 20 minutes, or until golden. Cool slightly, then remove the pies from the tin.

Makes 12

moroccan lamb mini pies

corn and bacon dip

2 corn cobs, husks and silks
   removed
250 g (9 oz) lean bacon,
   finely chopped

1 garlic clove, crushed
250 g (9 oz/1 cup) spreadable
   cream cheese
chopped chives, to garnish

Cut the kernels from from the corn cobs and cook, covered, in boiling water for about 10 minutes. Drain.

Meanwhile, cook the bacon in a non-stick frying pan until very crispy, then drain on paper towels.

Put the corn in a food processor with the garlic and mix until quite smooth. Add the cream cheese and process until well combined. Spoon into a serving dish and cool to room temperature. Sprinkle the bacon over the top and garnish with the chives.

Makes about 500 g (1 lb 2 oz/2 cups)

sweet potato chips

2 long orange sweet potatoes
vegetable oil, for deep-frying
sweet chilli sauce, to serve

Peel the sweet potatoes and slice them as thinly as possible.

Half-fill a deep saucepan with oil and heat to 180°C (350°F), or until a cube of bread dropped in the oil browns in 15 seconds. Add the sweet potato chips in small batches and cook until crisp and golden (don't overload the pan or they will stick together).

Remove with a slotted spoon and drain on paper towels. Lightly sprinkle with salt and serve immediately with sweet chilli sauce.

Makes about 80 chips

Flaky pastry is always tempting and when wrapped around this fiery mix will lead the most committed dieter to break the rules.

thai chicken sausage rolls

filling
200 g (7 oz) chicken breast fillet, roughly chopped
150 g (5^1/$_2$ oz) mild pancetta, chopped
1 garlic clove, crushed
3 spring onions (scallions), chopped
2 bird's eye chillies, seeded and finely chopped
2 tablespoons chopped coriander (cilantro) leaves
1 teaspoon fish sauce
1 egg
1 teaspoon grated fresh ginger

375 g (13 oz) block frozen puff pastry
1 egg yolk, lightly beaten
2 tablespoons sesame seeds
sweet chilli sauce, to serve

Preheat the oven to 180°C (350°F/Gas 4) and line a baking tray with baking paper.

To make the filling, put the chicken, pancetta, garlic, spring onion, chilli, coriander, fish sauce, egg and ginger in a food processor and process until just combined.

Roll out the pastry to a 30 x 40 cm (12 x 16 inch) rectangle. Cut in half lengthways. Take half the filling and, using floured hands, roll it into a long sausage shape and position along the long edge of one piece of pastry. Lightly brush the edges with water and fold over, pressing down to seal. Put the sealed edge underneath. Repeat with the remaining pastry and filling.

Using a sharp knife, cut the sausage rolls into 3 cm (1¼ inch) lengths; discard the end pieces. Brush the tops with egg yolk, then sprinkle with sesame seeds. Bake for 12–15 minutes, or until golden. Serve with sweet chilli sauce.

Makes 24

thai chicken sausage rolls

garlic lamb skewers

600 g (1 lb 5 oz) trimmed
    lamb steaks, cut into 2 cm
    (3/4 inch) cubes
6 garlic cloves, cut into thick
    slices

marinade
1 red chilli, seeded and chopped
2 garlic cloves, crushed
3 tablespoons oil, plus extra
    for brushing

Thread two lamb cubes and two slices of garlic alternately onto 24 small metal skewers.

To make the marinade, mix together the chilli, garlic and oil.

Heat a barbecue hot plate or chargrill pan (griddle) over high heat and lightly brush with oil. Cook the skewers for 4–5 minutes, turning and brushing occasionally with the marinade.

Makes 24

chilli vegetables

12 baby corn cobs, halved
12 shiitake mushrooms, halved
12 snowpeas (mangetout),
 halved

2 tablespoons oil, plus extra
 for brushing
1 garlic clove, crushed
1 tablespoon sweet chilli sauce

Soak 24 small wooden skewers in water for 1 hour. Thread the corn, mushrooms and snowpeas alternately onto the skewers.

Mix together the oil, garlic and sweet chilli sauce in a bowl and brush over the skewers.

Heat a barbecue hot plate or chargrill pan (griddle) over high heat and lightly brush with oil. Cook the skewers for 3–4 minutes, turning and brushing with the chilli oil during cooking.

Makes 24

dolmades

200 g (7 oz) packet vine leaves in brine
250 g (9 oz/1 cup) medium-grain rice
1 small onion, finely chopped
1 tablespoon olive oil
50 g (1¾ oz/⅓ cup) pine nuts, toasted
2 tablespoons currants
2 tablespoons chopped dill
2 tablespoons finely chopped mint
2 tablespoons finely chopped flat-leaf (Italian) parsley
4 tablespoons olive oil, extra
2 tablespoons lemon juice
500 ml (17 fl oz/2 cups) chicken or vegetable stock

Put the vine leaves in a bowl, cover with cold water and soak for about 15 minutes. Remove, pat dry and cut off any stems. Reserve five or six leaves; discard any with holes. Meanwhile, pour boiling water over the rice and soak for 10 minutes, then drain.

Put the rice, onion, olive oil, pine nuts, currants and herbs in a large bowl. Season with salt and pepper and mix well.

Lay some leaves vein-side-down on a flat surface. Put $1/2$ tablespoon of filling in the middle of each leaf, fold the stalk end over the filling, then the left and right sides into the middle, and finally roll firmly towards the tip. The dolmade should resemble a small fat cigar. Repeat with the remaining filling and leaves to make 48 dolmades.

Line the base of a large heavy-based saucepan or flameproof casserole with the reserved leaves. Drizzle with 1 tablespoon of the extra oil. Put the dolmades in the pan, tightly packing them in one layer. Pour the lemon juice and remaining oil over them.

Pour the stock over the dolmades and cover with an inverted plate to stop them moving while cooking. Bring to the boil, then reduce the heat and simmer gently, covered, for 45 minutes. Remove with a slotted spoon. Serve warm or cold.

Makes 48

garlic lamb skewers and dolmades

chilli con queso

2 green jalapeño chillies
30 g (1 oz) butter
1 onion, finely chopped

185 g (6$^1/_2$ oz/$^3/_4$ cup) sour cream
250 g (9 oz/2 cups) grated
    Cheddar cheese

Roast the chillies by holding them with tongs (one at a time) over a gas flame until well blackened. If you don't have a gas stove, cut the chillies in half, remove the seeds, flatten out and grill (broil) until the skin turns black. Put the chillies in a plastic bag and set aside to cool. Scrape away the skin, remove the seeds and finely chop the flesh.

Melt the butter in a small saucepan. Add the onion and cook over low heat for 5 minutes, or until softened and lightly golden. Stir in the chilli.

Add the sour cream and stir until the cream has warmed and thinned down slightly. Add the cheese and keep stirring until it has melted and the mixture is smooth. Serve warm.

Serves 6

corn chips

4 corn tortillas
vegetable oil, for deep-frying

Cut each corn tortilla into eight pieces.

Fill a heavy-based saucepan one-third full of oil and heat to 180°C (350°F), or until a cube of bread dropped in the oil browns in 15 seconds. Add the tortillas in batches and cook for 1–2 minutes, or until crisp and golden. Drain on paper towels, season with salt and serve.

Makes 32

herbed falafel with hummus and flatbread

2 teaspoons coriander seeds
2 teaspoons cumin seeds
110 g (3³/4 oz/¹/2 cup) dried chickpeas, soaked overnight
    and drained
195 g (7 oz/1¹/4 cups) frozen broad beans, thawed
2 tablespoons finely chopped onion
1 garlic clove, crushed
3 tablespoons chopped parsley
2 tablespoons chopped mint
2 tablespoons chopped coriander (cilantro) leaves
oil, for deep-frying
1 piece Lebanese (large pitta) bread
165 g (5³/4 oz/³/4 cup) ready-made or home-made hummus
    (see page 80)
4 tablespoons mustard cress
cayenne pepper, to serve

Toast the coriander and cumin seeds in a dry frying pan over low heat for 2–3 minutes, or until fragrant. Cool slightly then finely grind to a powder. Put the spice mix, chickpeas, broad beans, onion, garlic, parsley, mint, coriander and 1/2 teaspoon of salt in a food processor and purée. Using your hands, form the mixture into 24 flat rounds, about 4 cm (11/2 inches) in diameter. Put them on a tray, cover and refrigerate for 30 minutes.

Fill a deep heavy-based saucepan one-third full of oil and heat to 180°C (350°F), or until a cube of bread browns in 15 seconds. Tear the bread into quarters and deep-fry for 2–3 minutes, or until crisp and golden. Remove and drain on paper towels, then break into small pieces.

Reheat the oil and add the falafel in batches. Cook for 3–4 minutes, turning with a pair of tongs, until they turn dark golden. Remove and drain on crumpled paper towels. Top each falafel round with 1/2 teaspoon of hummus, a small piece of flatbread and some mustard cress. Sprinkle with cayenne pepper and serve.

Makes 24

herbed falafel with hummus and flatbread

dhal

250 g (9 oz/1 cup) red lentils, rinsed
1/4 teaspoon ground turmeric
1 tablespoon oil
1 tablespoon cumin seeds
1/2 teaspoon brown mustard seeds
1 onion, finely chopped
1 tablespoon grated fresh ginger
2 long green chillies, seeded and finely chopped
4 tablespoons lemon juice
2 tablespoons finely chopped coriander (cilantro) leaves

Put the lentils in a saucepan with 750 ml (26 fl oz/3 cups) of cold water. Bring to the boil, then reduce the heat and stir in the turmeric. Simmer, covered, for 20 minutes, or until tender.

Meanwhile, heat the oil in a saucepan over medium heat, add the cumin and mustard seeds and cook for 5–6 minutes, or until the seeds begin to pop. Stir in the onion, ginger and chilli and cook for 5 minutes, or until the onion is golden. Add the lentils and 125 ml (4 fl oz/1/2 cup) of water. Season with salt, reduce the heat and simmer for 10 minutes.

Spoon into a bowl, stir in the lemon juice and garnish with coriander leaves. Serve with spicy pappadams (see facing page).

Serves 6–8

spicy pappadams

3 green cardamom seeds
1 1/2 tablespoons coriander
   seeds
1 tablespoon cumin seeds
2 cloves
1 teaspoon black peppercorns
1 bay leaf, crushed

1 teaspoon ground mace
1/4 teaspoon ground cinnamon
pinch of chilli powder
oil, for deep-frying
24 large pappadams, broken
   into quarters

Toast the cardamom, coriander and cumin seeds, cloves, peppercorns and bay leaf in a dry frying pan over low heat for 2–3 minutes, or until richly fragrant. Cool for 5 minutes, then grind to a fine powder. Stir in the mace, cinnamon and chilli powder.

Fill a wide, large saucepan one-third full of oil and heat to 180°C (350°F), or until a cube of bread dropped in the oil browns in 15 seconds. Deep-fry the pieces of pappadam, a few at a time, until crisp and golden. Drain on crumpled paper towels and sprinkle with the spice mix while still hot.

Serves 6–8

mini roasted vegetable frittatas

4 tablespoons olive oil
3 French shallots, thinly sliced
3 garlic cloves, crushed
4 slender eggplants (aubergines), cut into 5 mm (1/4 inch) slices
2 zucchini (courgettes), cut into 5 mm (1/4 inch) slices
2 red capsicums (peppers), seeded and cut into 2–3 flat pieces
2 tablespoons finely chopped mint
1 handful basil, torn into small pieces
8 eggs
125 ml (4 fl oz/1/2 cup) cream
pinch of ground nutmeg
25 g (1 oz/1/4 cup) grated Parmesan cheese
mint leaves, extra, to garnish

Preheat the oven to 200°C (400°F/Gas 6). Lightly grease 24 x 5 cm (2 inch) non-stick tart holes. Heat the oil, shallots and garlic in a small saucepan over low heat for 1–2 minutes, or until just soft. Remove from the heat. Put the eggplant and zucchini slices in a single layer on a baking tray and brush both sides with the hot oil. Roast the vegetables for 10 minutes, then turn and cook for another 10 minutes, or until golden.

Put the capsicum strips, skin-side-up, under a hot grill (broiler) until the skin blackens and blisters. Cool in a plastic bag, then peel away the skin. Cut into 2 x 1 cm (3/4 x 1/2 inch) strips, then transfer to a bowl.

Remove the vegetables from the oven. Reduce the temperature to 180°C (350°F/Gas 4). Cut the vegetables into 2 x 1 cm (3/4 x 1/2 inch) strips and add to the bowl. Add the mint and basil, season and mix well.

Beat the eggs, cream, nutmeg and Parmesan together in a large bowl and season with salt and pepper.

Fill each tart hole one-third full of assorted pieces of vegetable mixture. Carefully pour the egg mixture in just short of the top. Distribute the remaining vegetables among the holes, pressing the pieces into the egg. Use the remaining egg mixture to top up the levels to equal heights. Transfer to the oven and bake for about 15 minutes, or until golden and set. The frittatas will rise a lot during cooking, but will sink once out of the oven. Cool for 5 minutes before turning out onto a wire rack. Top with a mint leaf and serve warm or cold.

Makes 24

mini roasted vegetable frittatas

spicy chicken goujons

3 chicken breast fillets, cut into
   thin strips
plain (all-purpose) flour, for
   coating
vegetable oil, for deep-frying

1/2 teaspoon ground turmeric
1/2 teaspoon ground coriander
1/2 teaspoon ground cumin
1/2 teaspoon chilli powder
sweet chilli sauce, to serve

Toss the chicken strips in the flour, shaking off the excess. Fill a deep heavy-based saucepan one-third full of oil and heat to 180°C (350°F), or until a cube of bread dropped in the oil browns in 15 seconds. Lower the chicken strips into the oil, a few at a time, and cook for 2–3 minutes, or until golden. Drain on paper towels and keep warm.

Mix together the turmeric, coriander, cumin, chilli powder and a teaspoon of salt. Toss the goujons in the mixture, shaking off the excess. Serve with sweet chilli sauce or a creamy dip.

Makes about 30

mushroom and prosciutto skewers

48 Swiss brown mushrooms
80 g (2³/₄ oz) butter
125 ml (4 fl oz/¹/₂ cup) port
18 slices of prosciutto, each cut
     into 4 pieces

Wipe the mushrooms with a damp cloth, then cut them in half. Melt the butter in a frying pan and add the mushrooms and a pinch of salt. Cook, stirring, over medium heat for 1 minute. Add the port and cook, stirring, until it evaporates completely. Remove from the heat.

Thread four pieces of mushroom and three rolled pieces of prosciutto alternately onto wooden skewers and serve.

Makes 24

stir-fried noodles with corn and peanuts

80 g (2³/4 oz/¹/2 cup) toasted peanuts
3 tablespoons coconut milk
2 tablespoons lime juice
¹/2 teaspoon ground turmeric
3 tablespoons oil
3 eggs, lightly beaten
125 g (4¹/2 oz) dried rice vermicelli
3 garlic cloves, crushed
1 tablespoon finely chopped fresh ginger
2 teaspoons shrimp paste (blachan)
6 spring onions (scallions), thinly sliced
400 g (14 oz) tin baby corn, drained, quartered lengthways
150 g (5¹/2 oz/1²/3 cups) bean sprouts
500 g (1 lb 2 oz) Chinese cabbage (wom bok), hard stems
    removed, thinly sliced
¹/2 small red capsicum (pepper), thinly sliced
1 large handful coriander (cilantro) leaves
1¹/2 tablespoons fish sauce
50 g (1³/4 oz/¹/3 cup) roasted peanuts, extra, chopped
small handful coriander (cilantro) leaves, extra
lime wedges, to serve

Mix the peanuts, coconut milk, lime juice and turmeric in a food processor until combined, but so the peanuts are only roughly chopped.

Heat 1 tablespoon of the oil in a large wok. Add the beaten egg and tilt the uncooked egg to the outer edge of the wok. Cook until firm, then remove from the wok and roll up firmly. Cut into thin slices.

Put the vermicelli in a bowl, cover with boiling water and leave to soak for 5 minutes. Drain and cut into short lengths with scissors.

Heat the remaining oil in the wok. Add the garlic, ginger and shrimp paste and stir-fry for 30 seconds, or until aromatic. Add the vegetables and stir-fry until tender. Add the vermicelli and stir-fry until heated through. Stir in the peanut mixture and stir-fry until well combined and heated through. Turn off the heat and gently stir in the omelette, coriander and fish sauce.

Divide the mixture among 18 mini takeaway boxes or small bowls and top with a sprinkling of the extra peanuts and coriander leaves. Serve with lime wedges and chopsticks.

Makes 18

stir-fried noodles with corn and peanuts

guacamole

2 large ripe avocados
2 tablespoons lime juice
1 tomato, seeded and finely diced
1 small red chilli, seeded and finely chopped
2 tablespoons finely diced red onion

1 1/2 tablespoons chopped coriander (cilantro) leaves
1 1/2 tablespoons sour cream
1 tablespoon olive oil
1/2 teaspoon ground cumin
pinch of cayenne pepper, plus extra, to serve

Put the avocado and lime juice in a large bowl, then mash. Stir in the tomato, chilli, onion, coriander, sour cream, olive oil and cumin. Season with cayenne pepper and some salt and pepper.

Spoon into a serving bowl and sprinkle with cayenne pepper. This is delicious served with tortilla shards (see facing page) or corn chips.

Serves 6–8

tortilla shards

2 tablespoons sweet paprika
1/4 teaspoon cayenne pepper
oil, for deep-frying
4 large flour tortillas, cut into
    12 long triangles

Combine the paprika and cayenne pepper in a small bowl. Fill a deep heavy-based saucepan one-third full of oil and heat to 180°C (350°F), or until a cube of bread dropped in the oil browns in 15 seconds. Drop the tortilla shards in the oil in batches and deep-fry until crisp.

Drain on crumpled paper towels and sprinkle lightly with the paprika mix while still hot. Try serving these with guacamole.

Makes 48

Committed vegetarians and meat-eaters alike will have to fight for their share of these yummy skewers.

chargrilled vegetable skewers

12 button mushrooms, cut in half
1 yellow capsicum (pepper), cut into 2 cm (3/4 inch) pieces
1 red capsicum (pepper), cut into 2 cm (3/4 inch) pieces
1 zucchini (courgette), cut into 2 cm (3/4 inch) pieces
1 small red onion, cut into 2 cm (3/4 inch) pieces
24 bay leaves
125 ml (4 fl oz/1/2 cup) olive oil
2 tablespoons lemon juice
1 garlic clove, crushed
2 teaspoons thyme leaves

concassé
1 tablespoon olive oil
1 small onion, finely chopped
1 garlic clove, crushed
425 g (15 oz) tin chopped tomatoes
4 tablespoons torn basil

Soak 24 wooden skewers in water for 1 hour. Thread each skewer with a piece of mushroom, yellow and red capsicum, zucchini, onion and a bay leaf, then put in a large, flat non-metallic dish and season well with salt and cracked black pepper.

Put the olive oil, lemon juice, garlic and thyme in a small bowl and mix together. Pour over the skewers and marinate for 20 minutes.

Meanwhile, to make the concassé, heat the oil in a small saucepan over medium heat, add the onion and cook for 5 minutes, or until soft. Stir in the garlic and cook for 30 seconds, then add the tomato. Simmer for 10–15 minutes, then add the basil.

Cook the skewers on a hot barbecue hotplate or chargrill pan (griddle) for 3 minutes on each side, or until golden, brushing occasionally with the marinade. Serve with the concassé.

Makes 24

chargrilled vegetable skewers

tzatziki

1 Lebanese (short) cucumber
2 garlic cloves, crushed
250 g (9 oz/1 cup) plain yoghurt
1 teaspoon white vinegar
1 teaspoon chopped dill
1 teaspoon chopped mint

Finely grate the cucumber and squeeze out the excess moisture. Transfer to a bowl with the garlic, yoghurt, vinegar, dill and mint, season to taste with salt and freshly ground black pepper and mix together well. Serve with spring onion flatbreads (see page 124).

Serves 6–8

taramasalata

4 slices white bread, crusts
   removed
4 tablespoons milk
200 g (7 oz) smoked cod or
   grey mullet roe
1 egg yolk

1 garlic clove, crushed
150–170 ml (5–5$^{1}/_{2}$ fl oz)
   olive oil
2 tablespoons lemon juice
1 tablespoon finely chopped
   parsley

Soak the bread in the milk for 5 minutes. Squeeze out the excess liquid and transfer to a food processor.

Add the roe, egg yolk and garlic and process until smooth. With the motor running, slowly pour in the oil, stopping when the mixture is thick and holds its form. Stir in the lemon juice and parsley. Season and add more lemon juice, if needed. If you prefer a deeper colour, you can add a few drops of red food colouring. Serve with spring onion flatbreads (see page 124).

Serves 6–8

Bursting with the sweet heat of spring onions, these little flatbreads are easy to make and utterly delicious for dipping.

spring onion flatbreads

2 teaspoons oil
170 g (6 oz/1 bunch) spring onions (scallions), thinly sliced
1 garlic clove, crushed
215 g (7¹/2 oz/1³/4 cups) plain (all-purpose) flour
1¹/2 tablespoons chopped coriander (cilantro) leaves
oil, for pan-frying

Heat the oil in a frying pan, add the spring onion and garlic and cook for 2–3 minutes, or until soft.

Combine the flour and 1 teaspoon of salt in a large bowl. Add the onion mixture and chopped coriander. Gradually stir in 250 ml (9 fl oz/1 cup) of boiling water, stopping when a loose dough forms. Knead the dough with floured hands for 1 1/2–2 minutes, or until smooth. Cover with plastic wrap and rest for 30 minutes.

Break off walnut-sized pieces of dough and roll out into 20 thin ovals. Fill a large frying pan with 2 cm (3/4 inch) of oil and heat over medium heat. When shimmering, cook the breads two or three at a time for about 25–30 seconds each side, or until crisp and golden. Drain on paper towels and serve warm.

Makes 20

spring onion flatbreads with
taramasalata and tzatziki

avocado and coriander dip

1 avocado
1 tablespoon sour cream
1 tablespoon lemon juice
1 tablespoon light olive oil

1 small tomato, seeded
1 large handful coriander
    (cilantro) leaves

Put the avocado, sour cream, lemon juice, oil, tomato and coriander in a food processor and mix until smooth. Season with salt and pepper.

Transfer to a bowl, lay plastic wrap directly onto the surface of the dip (to prevent a skin forming) and keep refrigerated until ready to use. Try to make this dip close to serving time, so it doesn't discolour.

Serves 6–8

vegetable chips

500 g (1 lb 2 oz) orange sweet
    potato
500 g (1 lb 2 oz) parsnip

500 g (1 lb 2 oz) beetroot
vegetable oil, for deep-frying

Run a vegetable peeler along the length of the sweet potato and parsnip
to make thin ribbons. Cut the beetroot into thin slices.

Fill a deep heavy-based saucepan half-full of oil and heat to 190°C (375°F),
or until a cube of bread dropped in the oil browns in 10 seconds. Cook
the vegetables in batches for about 30 seconds, or until golden and crisp,
turning with tongs if necessary. Drain on crumpled paper towels, then
season with salt and serve hot.

Serves 8–10

Easy to pack and utterly delicious — the classic pairing of spicy lamb and cool yoghurt makes koftas perfect picnic fare.

spicy koftas

yoghurt dip
1 small tomato, peeled, seeded and finely chopped
1/2 Lebanese (short) cucumber, peeled and finely
   chopped
1 garlic clove, crushed
1 tablespoon chopped mint
125 g (4 oz/1/2 cup) plain yoghurt

500 g (1 lb 2 oz) minced (ground) lamb
1 small onion, finely chopped
1 garlic clove, crushed
1 teaspoon ground coriander
1 teaspoon ground cumin
1/4 teaspoon ground cinnamon
1/2 teaspoon seeded and finely chopped red chilli

1 teaspoon tomato paste (purée)
1 tablespoon chopped mint
1 tablespoon chopped coriander (cilantro) leaves
oil, for pan-frying

To make the yoghurt dip, mix together all the ingredients and spoon into a small bowl. Cover and keep in the refrigerator until ready to serve.

Put the lamb, onion, garlic, coriander, cumin, cinnamon, chilli, tomato paste, mint and coriander in a large bowl and mix well with your hands. Season well, then roll into small balls (about 1^1/$_2$ teaspoons each).

Heat a little oil in a large heavy-based frying pan over medium heat. Add the koftas in batches and cook until well browned all over and cooked through. Drain on crumpled paper towels. Skewer each kofta with a cocktail stick and serve with the yoghurt dip.

Makes 45

vegetable chips

white bean dip

2 x 400 g (14 oz) tins lima or
    cannellini beans, drained
    and rinsed
125 ml (4 fl oz/1/2 cup) olive oil
4 tablespoons lemon juice

3 garlic cloves, finely chopped
1 tablespoon finely chopped
    rosemary

Put the beans in a food processor with the oil, lemon juice, garlic and rosemary and 1 teaspoon of salt. Process until smooth, then season with cracked black pepper.

Serves 6–8

potato skins

5 large potatoes
oil, for deep-frying

Preheat the oven to 210°C (415°F/Gas 6–7). Scrub the potatoes and pat dry with paper towels but do not peel. Prick each potato with a fork and bake for 1 hour, or until the skins are crisp and the flesh is soft. Turn once during cooking.

Leave the potatoes to cool, then halve them and scoop out the flesh, leaving a thin layer of potato in each shell. Cut each half into three wedges.

Fill a heavy-based saucepan one-third full of oil and heat to 180°C (350°F), or until a cube of bread dropped in the oil browns in 15 seconds. Cook the potato skins in batches for 2–3 minutes, or until crisp. Drain on paper towels. Season well and serve with a creamy dip or a salsa.

Makes 30

Crunchy, salty and loaded with aromatic herbs, these grissini are wonderfully moreish and perfect for dining *al fresco*.

herb grissini

7 g sachet dried yeast
1 teaspoon sugar
500 g (1 lb 2 oz/4 cups) plain (all-purpose) flour
3 tablespoons olive oil
1 1/2 large handfuls flat-leaf (Italian) parsley, chopped
3 tablespoons chopped basil
2 teaspoons sea salt flakes

Combine the yeast, sugar and 315 ml (11 fl oz/1 1/4 cups) of warm water in a small bowl and leave in a warm place for 5–10 minutes, or until foamy.

Sift the flour and 1 teaspoon of salt into a bowl. Stir in the yeast mixture and oil to form a dough, adding more water if necessary. Gather into a ball and turn out onto a lightly floured surface. Knead for 10 minutes, or until soft and elastic. Add the herbs, and knead for 1–2 minutes to incorporate evenly. Put the dough in a lightly oiled bowl and cover with plastic wrap. Leave in a warm place for 1 hour, or until doubled in volume.

Preheat the oven to 230°C (450°F/Gas 8) and lightly grease two large baking trays. Punch down the dough and knead for 1 minute. Divide into 24 portions, and roll each portion into a 30 cm (12 inch) long stick. Put the sticks on the trays and lightly brush with water. Sprinkle with the salt flakes and bake for 10 minutes, or until crisp and golden.

Makes 24

herb grissini

creamy herb mini quiches

2 sheets ready-rolled shortcrust
   pastry
2 eggs, beaten
2 tablespoons milk
125 ml (4 fl oz/1/2 cup) cream
2 teaspoons chopped chives

1 teaspoon chopped dill
1 teaspoon chopped thyme
1 teaspoon chopped parsley
2 tablespoons grated Parmesan
   cheese

Preheat the oven to 200°C (400°F/Gas 6). Lightly grease 24 mini tart tins. Lay the pastry sheets on a work surface and cut out 24 shapes to fit the tins. Line the tins with pastry.

Mix together the beaten egg, milk, cream, chives, dill, thyme and parsley. Pour into the pastry cases and sprinkle with the grated Parmesan. Bake for 15–20 minutes, or until puffed and golden. Remove from the tins while warm and cool on wire racks.

Makes 24

smoked salmon mini quiches

2 sheets ready-rolled shortcrust
    pastry
100 g (3¹/2 oz) cream cheese
3 tablespoons cream
2 eggs

100 g (3¹/2 oz) smoked salmon,
    finely chopped
3 tablespoons salmon roe
small dill sprigs, to garnish

Preheat the oven to 200°C (400°F/Gas 6). Lightly grease 24 mini tart tins. Lay the pastry sheets on a work surface and cut out 24 shapes to fit the tins. Line the tins with pastry.

Put the cream cheese, cream and eggs in a food processor and mix together, then add some cracked black pepper, to taste. Sprinkle a little smoked salmon into each pastry case, then pour the cream cheese mixture over the top. Bake for 15–20 minutes, or until puffed and golden. Remove from the tins while warm and cool on wire racks. Top with a little salmon roe and a sprig of dill before serving.

Makes 24

Sweet, tender caramelized onion is a natural partner for salty, crispy bacon, proving opposites really do attract.

caramelized onion and bacon mini quiches

2 sheets ready-rolled shortcrust pastry
2 teaspoons oil
1 large onion, finely chopped
125 g (4^1/$_2$ oz) bacon, finely chopped
3 teaspoons wholegrain mustard
2 eggs
125 ml (4 fl oz/^{1}/$_2$ cup) milk

Preheat the oven to 200°C (400°F/Gas 6). Lightly grease 24 mini tart tins. Lay the pastry sheets on a work surface and cut out 24 shapes to fit the tins. Line the tins with pastry.

Heat the oil in a large saucepan over low–medium heat. Add the onion and cook for about 30 minutes, or until golden (caramelized onion needs to be slow-cooked to bring out the sweetness, so don't rush this step). Transfer to a bowl to cool.

Add the bacon to the pan and cook until crisp. Add to the onion, stir in the mustard and season to taste with pepper. Spoon a small amount into each pastry case.

Beat the eggs with the milk and pour over the onion and bacon mixture. Bake for 15–20 minutes, or until puffed and golden. Remove from the tins while warm and cool on wire racks.

Makes 24

smoked salmon mini quiches

baba ganouj

2 eggplants (aubergines)
   (about 1 kg/2 lb 4 oz)
4 tablespoons lemon juice
2 tablespoons tahini
1 1/2 tablespoons olive oil
3 garlic cloves, crushed

1/2 teaspoon ground cumin
pinch of cayenne pepper
1 tablespoon finely chopped
   flat-leaf (Italian) parsley
black olives, to garnish

Preheat the oven to 200°C (400°F/Gas 6). Pierce the eggplants a few times with a fork, then cook over an open flame for about 5 minutes, or until the skin is black and blistered all over. Transfer the eggplant to a roasting tin and bake for 35–40 minutes, or until soft and wrinkled.

Put the eggplant in a colander over a bowl to drain off any bitter juices and leave for 30 minutes, or until cool. Carefully peel off the skin and put the flesh in a food processor with the lemon juice, tahini, oil, garlic, cumin and cayenne pepper. Process until smooth and creamy. Season to taste with salt and stir in the chopped parsley. Spread onto a serving plate and garnish with a few olives.

Serves 6–8

honey mustard chicken drumettes

4 tablespoons oil

3 tablespoons honey

3 tablespoons soy sauce

3 tablespoons Dijon mustard

3 tablespoons lemon juice

4 garlic cloves, crushed

24 chicken drumettes (wings with the wing tip removed)

Put the oil, honey, soy sauce, mustard, lemon juice and garlic in a large non-metallic dish and mix together well.

Trim the chicken of excess fat, then add to the dish and toss until well coated in the marinade. Cover and refrigerate for at least 2 hours, or preferably overnight, turning 2–3 times.

Preheat the oven to 200°C (400°F/Gas 6). Put the drumettes on a wire rack over a foil-lined baking tray. Bake, turning and brushing with the marinade three or four times, for 45 minutes, or until golden brown and cooked. Serve immediately with napkins for sticky fingers.

Makes 24

These crunchy little chicken strips mix the bite of nutty
macadamias with the spicy sweetness of mango salsa.

macadamia-crusted chicken strips with mango salsa

12 chicken tenderloins
seasoned plain (all-purpose) flour, for coating
2 eggs, lightly beaten
240 g (8³/4 oz/1¹/2 cups) macadamias,
    finely chopped
160 g (5³/4 oz/2 cups) fresh breadcrumbs
oil, for deep-frying

mango salsa
1 small mango, very finely diced
2 tablespoons finely diced red onion
2 tablespoons roughly chopped coriander
    (cilantro) leaves
1 green chilli, seeded and finely chopped
1 tablespoon lime juice

Cut the chicken into strips and dust with the flour. Dip the strips in the egg, then coat them in the combined nuts and breadcrumbs. Refrigerate for at least 30 minutes to firm up.

To make the salsa, combine all the ingredients in a small bowl and season to taste with salt and pepper.

Fill a large heavy-based saucepan one-third full of oil and heat to 180°C (350°F), or until a cube of bread dropped in the oil browns in 15 seconds. Cook the chicken strips in batches for 2–3 minutes, or until golden brown all over, taking care not to burn the nuts. Drain well on crumpled paper towels. Serve warm with the salsa.

Makes about 24

macadamia-crusted chicken strips with mango salsa

classic brownies

125 g (4½ oz/1 cup) plain (all-purpose) flour
½ teaspoon baking powder
150 g (5½ oz) good-quality dark chocolate
90 g (3¼ oz) unsalted butter

2 eggs, lightly beaten
170 g (6 oz/¾ cup) caster (superfine) sugar
1 teaspoon vanilla essence
100 g (3½ oz) milk chocolate bits (chips)

Preheat the oven to 180°C (350°F/Gas 4). Lightly grease a shallow 20 cm (8 inch) square cake tin and line the base and sides with baking paper, leaving the paper hanging over two opposite sides.

Sift the flour and baking powder together. Chop the chocolate and butter into small even-sized pieces and put in a heatproof bowl. Bring a saucepan of water to the boil, then remove from the heat. Sit the bowl over the saucepan, making sure the bowl does not touch the water. Leave, stirring occasionally, until the chocolate and butter have melted. Cool slightly.

Put the eggs, sugar and vanilla essence in a bowl and beat with electric beaters for 2 minutes, or until pale and thick. Stir in the melted chocolate mixture. Fold in the flour with a metal spoon until combined, then add the chocolate bits and mix well. Spoon into the tin and bake for 30 minutes, or until a skewer inserted in the centre comes out clean. Leave in the tin for 10 minutes, then cool completely on a wire rack. Cut into squares.

Makes 16 pieces

pecan brownies

125 g (4¹/₂ oz) good-quality
    dark chocolate
90 g (3¹/₄ oz) unsalted butter,
    softened
230 g (8 oz/1 cup) caster
    (superfine) sugar
1 teaspoon vanilla essence

2 eggs
85 g (3 oz/²/₃ cup) plain
    (all-purpose) flour
30 g (1 oz/¹/₄ cup) cocoa powder
¹/₂ teaspoon baking powder
125 g (4¹/₂ oz/1 cup) roughly
    chopped pecans

Preheat the oven to 180°C (350°F/Gas 4). Lightly grease a shallow 17 cm (6¹/₂ inch) square cake tin and line the base and sides with baking paper, leaving the paper hanging over two opposite sides.

Chop the chocolate into small even-sized pieces and put in a heatproof bowl. Bring a saucepan of water to the boil, then remove from the heat. Sit the bowl over the saucepan, making sure the bowl does not touch the water. Leave, stirring occasionally, until melted. Cool slightly.

Beat the butter, sugar and vanilla with electric beaters until thick and creamy. Add the eggs one at a time, beating well after each addition. Stir in the chocolate. Sift the flour, cocoa and baking powder and fold in with a metal spoon, then fold in the pecans. Spoon into the tin and smooth the surface. Bake for 30–35 minutes, or until firm and it comes away from the sides of the tin. Cool in the tin, remove and cut into squares.

Makes 16 pieces

passionfruit and coconut cheese slice

100 g (3$\frac{1}{2}$ oz/$\frac{2}{3}$ cup) blanched almonds
125 g (4$\frac{1}{2}$ oz/1 cup) plain (all-purpose) flour
1 teaspoon baking powder
100 g (3$\frac{1}{2}$ oz) unsalted butter, chopped
115 g (4 oz/$\frac{1}{2}$ cup) caster (superfine) sugar
2 eggs, plus 1 egg yolk
25 g (1 oz/$\frac{1}{4}$ cup) desiccated coconut
600 g (1 lb 5 oz/2$\frac{1}{3}$ cups) cream cheese
125 ml (4 fl oz/$\frac{1}{2}$ cup) coconut milk
3 teaspoons vanilla essence
$\frac{1}{2}$ teaspoon lemon juice
170 g (6 oz/$\frac{3}{4}$ cup) caster (superfine) sugar, extra
90 g (3$\frac{1}{4}$ oz/$\frac{3}{4}$ cup) icing (confectioners') sugar
40 g (1$\frac{1}{2}$ oz) unsalted butter, extra, softened
1 tablespoon cornflour (cornstarch)
2 tablespoons strained passionfruit juice
40 g (1$\frac{1}{2}$ oz/$\frac{3}{4}$ cup) flaked coconut

Finely chop the almonds in a food processor. Sift the flour and baking powder into a large bowl. Add the butter and rub into the flour with your fingertips until it resembles breadcrumbs. Stir in the almonds and sugar.

Make a well in the centre and add the egg yolk. Mix with a flat-bladed knife, using a cutting action, until the mixture comes together in beads. Add 2 tablespoons of cold water if needed. Gently gather the mixture together and put on a lightly floured work surface. Shape into a ball, flatten slightly, then wrap in plastic wrap and refrigerate for 30 minutes.

Preheat the oven to 170°C (325°F/Gas 3). Lightly grease a 27 x 18 x 5 cm (10³/4 x 7 x 2 inch) tin and line with baking paper, hanging over the two long sides. Roll out the dough to fit the base of the tin and press in evenly. Sprinkle the coconut over the base and lightly press it in. Bake for about 10 minutes, then cool for 10 minutes.

Combine the cream cheese and whole eggs in a food processor. Add the coconut milk, vanilla, lemon juice and extra sugar and blend until smooth. Pour over the base and bake for 40 minutes, or until firm. Cool in the tin.

Mix the icing sugar and extra butter with a wooden spoon until smooth. Stir in the cornflour, then gradually add the passionfruit juice. Mix until smooth. Using a 5 cm (2 inch) cutter, cut out 12 rounds from the cooled cake. Spread the icing on thickly and top with the flaked coconut.

Makes 12 pieces

passionfruit and coconut cheese slice

teatime A delicious combination of elegance and sophistication, tea is back on the menu after years in the wilderness. Sandwiches and scones, chocolates and cakes, scaled down and layered up,

provide for indulgent grazing. Tea and loads of Champagne are all you need to complete the menu for your baby shower, hen's night or any other occasion that calls for a gathering of the girls.

There is a defined order and spread of delights associated with the classic afternoon tea that provides a wonderful framework within which to plan the menu. There should be a range of savouries, cakes, biscuits and scones to achieve the full effect of a sumptuous tea. Traditional menus served up an array of sandwiches, usually cucumber, roast beef and smoked salmon, then a selection of miniature cakes, biscuits and scones with jam and cream. From this basis you can add a deliciously wide range of recipes — feel free to serve whatever you wish, but the rule is to keep it small and delicate. Serving it up is half the fun, and a tea for the girls is the ideal time to indulge your feminine side. Flowers, napkins, crystal and silver all set the tone for an afternoon of quiet luxury. A mismatched set of fine china teacups in old-fashioned floral prints makes for an unconventional yet elegant look. For those of you with a secret penchant for doilies, there is no better time to indulge. Tea, coffee, hot chocolate and perhaps Champagne are all you need to complete the meal. Offer a range of loose teas and make sure you have a couple of teapots to hand; this is not the time for a tea bag in a chipped mug, it's more about putting on the Ritz at home. Elegant dainties, fortifying brews and conversation are the key pleasures of a classic afternoon tea.

161

smoked trout tea sandwiches

250 g (9 oz/1 cup) softened
   cream cheese
24 thin slices brown bread
1 large telegraph (long)
   cucumber, cut into
   wafer-thin slices

400 g (14 oz) good-quality
   smoked trout
2 tablespoons roughly chopped
   dill
lemon wedges, to garnish

Spread the cream cheese on the bread slices. Arrange a single layer of cucumber on half the bread slices. Layer the trout over the cucumber, then top with the other bread slices.

Remove the crusts, then cut into four triangles. Arrange the sandwiches long-edge-down on a platter to form a pyramid. Brush one side of the pyramid with softened cream cheese, then sprinkle with dill. Garnish with the lemon wedges and serve.

Makes 48

lemon sandwiches with prawns

1½ thin-skinned lemons
60 g (2¼ oz) butter
10 slices multi-grain bread

1 kg (2 lb 4 oz) cooked king
prawns (shrimp), peeled and
deveined, tails intact

Wash and dry the lemons and slice very finely. Butter the bread slices.
Put a layer of lemon slices on top of five pieces of bread, then sandwich
with the remaining bread slices. Cut each sandwich into eight triangles.
Remove the crusts and serve with the prawns.

Makes 40

marinated trout and cucumber tarts

filling
300 g (10$^{1}/_2$ oz) ocean trout fillet
3 tablespoons lemon juice
2 tablespoons extra virgin olive oil
$^{1}/_2$ small Lebanese (short) cucumber, finely chopped
2 spring onions (scallions), finely sliced
24 baby English spinach leaves
24 dill sprigs

125 g (4$^{1}/_2$ oz/1 cup) plain (all-purpose) flour
2 tablespoons grated Parmesan cheese
75 g (2$^{1}/_2$ oz) chilled butter, cubed
1 egg, lightly beaten

To make the filling, remove the skin from the trout, then, using kitchen tweezers, take out the bones. Freeze the fish in plastic wrap for about 1 hour. Whisk the lemon juice and oil in a bowl. Cut the fish into 3 x 1 cm (1$^{1}/_4$ x $^{1}/_2$ inch) strips and add to the lemon marinade. Leave, covered, at room temperature for 20 minutes, or until the fish turns opaque (in summer, refrigerate — this will take a little longer). Drain off most of the marinade, leaving just enough to moisten the fish. Add the cucumber and spring onion. Season.

Sift the flour and a pinch of salt into a large bowl and add the Parmesan and butter. Rub in with your fingertips until the mixture resembles fine breadcrumbs. Make a well. Stir in the egg with a flat-bladed knife until the mixture comes together in beads. Turn onto a lightly floured surface and gather into a ball. Wrap in plastic wrap and refrigerate for 30 minutes.

Preheat the oven to 200°C (400°F/Gas 6). Lightly grease 24 round-based tart tins. Roll out the pastry to about 2 mm ($^1/_{16}$ inch) thick and cut out 24 x 6 cm ($2^1/_2$ inch) rounds (the pastry cases will be smaller than the tins). Prick the pastry lightly with a fork and bake for 8 minutes, or until golden. Remove from the tins and set aside to cool. Put a spinach leaf in each tart case and spoon on 1 level tablespoon of filling. Top with a dill sprig.

Makes 24

marinated trout and cucumber tarts

chicken and guacamole squares

guacamole
2 avocados
1 tablespoon mayonnaise
1 teaspoon chopped seeded
    chilli
1 tablespoon lemon juice
1 small tomato, chopped
1/2 red onion, finely chopped

8 slices wholemeal bread,
    crusts removed
250 g (9 oz) sliced smoked
    chicken breast
30 g (1 oz/1 cup) snowpea
    (mangetout) sprouts,
    trimmed
25 g (1 oz) butter

To make the guacamole, mash the avocados with the mayonnaise, chilli, lemon juice, tomato and onion.

Spread the guacamole over four slices of bread and top with the chicken slices. Add the snowpea sprouts. Butter the remaining bread slices and press onto the sprouts. Cut each sandwich into four squares and serve.

Makes 16

turkey and brie triangles

8 slices bread, crusts removed
$1^1/_2$ tablespoons cranberry sauce
125 g ($4^1/_2$ oz) sliced turkey
   breast

125 g ($4^1/_2$ oz) Brie cheese,
   sliced
4 butter lettuce leaves

Spread four slices of bread with cranberry sauce. Arrange the turkey breast, Brie and lettuce leaves over the sauce, then sandwich with the remaining bread slices. Cut each sandwich into four triangles and serve.

Makes 16

Herbs picked straight from the garden are more aromatic and impart a greater perfume to a dish — there is no substitute.

herbed crepe rolls

2 eggs
85 g (3 oz/^{2}/$_3$ cup) plain (all-purpose) flour
200 ml (7 fl oz) milk
^{1}/$_2$ teaspoon baking powder
30 g (1 oz) butter, melted
20 g (^{3}/$_4$ oz) butter, extra
3 tablespoons roughly chopped dill
2 tablespoons sliced spring onions (scallions)
100 g (3^1/$_2$ oz) shaved leg ham
130 g (4^1/$_2$ oz/1 cup) grated Jarlsberg cheese

Beat the eggs in a bowl and add the flour and milk a little at a time. Beat to form a smooth batter. Add the baking powder and melted butter, beat to combine, then refrigerate for 30 minutes. Just before using, remove from the refrigerator and beat again to combine.

Heat 1 teaspoon of the extra butter in a non-stick frying pan over medium heat. When it begins to sizzle, pour in a quarter of the batter and swirl around the bottom of the pan to make a crepe with a diameter of about 20 cm (8 inches). Sprinkle on a quarter of the dill and spring onion, and cook for 2–3 minutes, or until bubbles appear on the surface. Carefully turn the crepe over and cook for 1 minute before turning over once more. Remove and repeat with the remaining butter, batter, dill and spring onion to make four crepes.

Fill the crepes with the ham and grated cheese and roll up to form a log. Return to the pan and cook over low heat for 4–5 more minutes, turning every minute or so, to melt the cheese inside. Remove, cool slightly and slice diagonally to serve.

Makes 24

herbed crepe roll

mini focaccia with roasted vegetables

2 red capsicums (peppers), cut
    into 3 cm (1¼ inch) pieces
2 yellow capsicums (peppers), cut
    into 3 cm (1¼ inch) pieces
3 slender eggplants (aubergines),
    cut into 1 cm (½ inch) rounds
2 large zucchini (courgettes), cut
    into 1 cm (½ inch) rounds
1 red onion, thinly sliced

4 tablespoons extra virgin
    olive oil
3 garlic cloves, crushed
12 mini focaccias, split in half
3 tablespoons ready-made
    or home-made pesto
3 large fresh bocconcini
    cheese, sliced

Preheat the oven to 200°C (400°F/Gas 6). Put all the vegetables in a large roasting tin with the oil and garlic, season with salt and cracked black pepper and toss together well. Roast for 25 minutes, or until cooked.

Spread each focaccia half with ½ teaspoon of pesto. Arrange the roasted vegetables over each base, top with two slices of bocconcini, then sandwich with the lids. Toast on both sides on a hot chargrill pan (griddle).

Cut each focaccia in half (or quarters, depending on the size of the focaccia), then wrap a wide band of paper around the middle of the sandwiches. Serve warm.

Makes 24

sweet potato rosti

3 orange sweet potatoes,
    unpeeled
2 teaspoons cornflour
    (cornstarch)

40 g (1^1/$_2$ oz) butter
150 g (5^1/$_2$ oz) mozzarella cheese,
    cut into 30 cubes

Boil the sweet potatoes until almost cooked, but still firm. Set aside to cool, then peel and coarsely grate into a bowl. Add the cornflour and ^{1}/$_2$ teaspoon of salt and toss lightly to combine.

Melt a little of the butter in a frying pan over low heat. Put teaspoons of the potato mixture in the pan and press a cube of cheese in the centre of each mound. Top with another teaspoon of potato and gently flatten to form rough circles. Increase the heat to medium and cook for 3 minutes on each side, or until golden. Remove and drain on paper towels. Repeat with remaining potato mixture and mozzarella cubes. Serve hot.

Makes 30

Sharp, pungent Stilton lends a serious bite to these delectable scones, yet is softened by the deep sweetness of the syrupy figs.

mini scones with ham and port figs

scones
2 cups (250 g/9 oz) plain (all-purpose) flour
3 teaspoons baking powder
110 g (3³/₄ oz) chilled butter
100 g (3¹/₂ oz) Stilton cheese
2 tablespoons chopped chives
185 ml (6 fl oz/³/₄ cup) milk

250 ml (9 fl oz/1 cup) port
6 large dried figs, stems removed
1 teaspoon sugar
2 teaspoons Dijon mustard
4 tablespoons sour cream
150 g (5¹/₂ oz) shaved ham
garlic chives, to garnish

To make the scones, sift the flour, baking powder and ³/₄ teaspoon of salt into a large bowl. Coarsely grate the butter and cheese into the flour and rub in with your fingertips until the mixture resembles coarse breadcrumbs. Stir in the chives. Pour in the milk and mix with a flat-bladed knife until the mixture comes together in beads. Turn onto a floured surface and press into a ball.

On a floured surface, roll the dough into a 15 x 25 cm (6 x 10 inch) rectangle. With the long edge of the dough facing you, fold in both ends so they meet in the centre, then fold the dough in half widthways. Roll again into a 15 x 25 cm (6 x 10 inch) rectangle, about 1 cm (^{1}/$_2$ inch) thick. Cut rounds close together with a 4 cm (1^1/$_2$ inch) cutter. Push the scraps together and roll and cut as before. Arrange the scones 2.5 cm (1 inch) apart on a baking tray and refrigerate for 20 minutes. Preheat the oven to 220°C (425°F/Gas 7). Bake for 10–12 minutes, or until lightly browned.

Heat the port, figs and sugar in a small saucepan. Bring to the boil, then reduce the heat and simmer for 15 minutes. Remove the figs. Simmer the liquid for 3 minutes, until reduced and syrupy. Cut each fig into 3 pieces.

Cut the top off the scones and discard. Combine the mustard and sour cream and spread over the scone bottoms. Top with a folded piece of ham. Put a piece of fig on top and drizzle with fig syrup. Top with garlic chives.

Makes 18

mini focaccia with roasted vegetables

mini scones with ham and port figs

pan-fried cheese sandwiches

20 thick slices white bread,
    crusts removed
2–3 tablespoons Dijon mustard
10 slices Cheddar cheese
oil, for pan-frying

plain (all-purpose) flour,
    for coating
3 eggs, lightly beaten
watercress, to garnish

Spread the bread with mustard, put a slice of cheese on top of half the slices, then sandwich with the other bread slices.

Heat a little oil in a frying pan. Dust the sandwiches lightly with flour and dip quickly into the beaten egg.

Add the sandwiches to the pan and cook on both sides until golden. Drain well on paper towels, cut each sandwich into quarters and garnish with watercress. Serve hot.

Makes 40

chicken, rocket and walnut sandwiches

oil, for pan-frying
750 g (1 lb 10 oz) chicken
    thigh fillets
250 g (9 oz/1 cup) whole-egg
    mayonnaise
2 celery sticks, finely chopped

60 g (2$\frac{1}{4}$ oz/$\frac{1}{2}$ cup) chopped
    walnuts
20 slices bread, crusts removed
40 g (1$\frac{1}{2}$ oz/1$\frac{1}{4}$ cups) rocket
    (arugula) leaves, trimmed

Heat a little oil in a frying pan, add the chicken fillets in batches and cook
for 6 minutes, or until cooked through. Cool, then finely chop.

Mix the chicken with the mayonnaise, celery and walnuts. Season to taste
with salt and pepper.

Spread the chicken mixture over 10 slices of bread, top with a few rocket
leaves and sandwich with the remaining bread slices. Cut each sandwich
into three fingers and serve.

Makes 30

herbed pikelets with pear and blue cheese topping

125 g (4 1/2 oz/1 cup) self-raising flour
2 eggs, lightly beaten
125 ml (4 fl oz/1/2 cup) milk
2 tablespoons finely chopped parsley
2 teaspoons finely chopped sage
cooking oil spray, for pan-frying

pear and blue cheese topping
100 g (3 1/2 oz) Blue Castello or other creamy blue cheese
75 g (2 1/2 oz) cream cheese
2 teaspoons brandy
1 large, ripe green-skinned pear
30 g (1 oz/1/4 cup) finely chopped toasted walnuts
1/2 lemon
1 1/2 tablespoons finely chopped chives

Sift the flour into a bowl and make a well in the centre. Gradually add the combined eggs and milk, mixing the flour in slowly. When the flour is incorporated, add the parsley and sage and season well with salt and cracked black pepper. Whisk until a smooth batter forms.

Heat a large non-stick frying pan over medium heat and spray with cooking oil spray. Drop heaped teaspoons of batter into the pan and flatten them a little to give 5 cm (2 inch) rounds. Cook until bubbles appear on the surface of the pikelets, then turn and brown the other side. Lift onto a wire rack to cool.

To make the topping, beat the cheeses and brandy together until smooth. Season with pepper. Cut the pear in half. Peel and core one half of it, then cut it into 5 mm (1/4 inch) dice, leaving the rest of the pear untouched. Stir the diced pear into the cheese mixture along with the walnuts.

Core the other half of the pear but do not peel it. Cut it into thin slices along its length (so that each slice has one border with the skin on). Cut these into 2 cm (3/4 inch) triangles with one slightly curved side having green skin. Squeeze some lemon juice over the cut surfaces to prevent discolouration.

Pile 1 teaspoon of topping in the centre of each pikelet and flatten it slightly to cover most of the surface. Arrange two of the pear triangles on top in a row, overlapping one another. Sprinkle with chives.

Makes 36

herbed pikelets with pear and blue cheese topping

basic tartlet cases

250 g (9 oz/2 cups) plain
    (all-purpose) flour
125 g (4^1/2 oz) chilled butter,
    chopped
1 egg

Preheat the oven to 200°C (400°F/Gas 6). Lightly grease 24 x 5 cm (2 inch) mini tartlet tins. Sift the flour into a large bowl and rub the butter in with your fingertips until the mixture resembles fine breadcrumbs. Make a well in the centre, add the egg and mix with a flat-bladed knife, using a cutting action until it comes together in beads. If the dough seems too dry, add a little cold water. Press the dough into a ball on a lightly floured surface, then wrap it in plastic wrap and refrigerate for 30 minutes.

Roll out the dough between two sheets of baking paper to a thickness of 2 mm (^{1}/16 inch) and cut out 24 rounds with an 8 cm (3^1/4 inch) cutter. Press the rounds into the prepared tins. Prick the bases with a fork and bake for 6–8 minutes, or until dry and golden. If they puff up, use a clean tea towel to press out any air pockets. Allow to cool before filling with the topping of your choice.

Makes 24

cherry tomato and bocconcini tartlets

300 g (10½ oz) cherry
   tomatoes, quartered
2 tablespoons olive oil
1 garlic clove, crushed
200 g (7 oz) baby bocconcini
   cheese, quartered
80 g (2¾ oz/½ cup) pitted
   Kalamata olives, chopped

1 tablespoon extra virgin
   olive oil
3 tablespoons olive oil, extra
24 small basil leaves
24 cooked tartlet cases
   (see facing page)

Preheat the oven to 200°C (400°F/Gas 6). Combine the tomatoes, olive oil and garlic in a roasting tin and bake for 15 minutes, or until the tomatoes are shrivelled but still firm. Allow to cool, then transfer to a bowl. Add the bocconcini, olives and extra virgin olive oil, then season and gently toss.

Heat the extra olive oil in a frying pan over high heat. Add the basil leaves in batches and pan-fry for 10–15 seconds, or until crisp. Drain.

Spoon the tomato and bocconcini filling into the tartlet cases and garnish with a basil leaf.

Makes 24

Don't hurry the onions as it takes time to bring out their true sweetness; but, like all good things, they're worth the wait.

caramelized red onion and feta tartlets

1¹/₂ tablespoons olive oil
2 large red onions, finely chopped
2 teaspoons chopped thyme
3 sheets ready-rolled shortcrust pastry
70 g (2¹/₂ oz) feta cheese, crumbled
2 eggs, lightly beaten
125 ml (4 fl oz/¹/₂ cup) cream

Preheat the oven to 180°C (350°F/Gas 4). Heat the oil in a frying pan (don't use a non-stick one or the onion won't caramelize). Add the onion and cook over medium–low heat, stirring occasionally, for 30 minutes, or until dark gold. Stir in the thyme, then transfer to a bowl to cool.

Grease 24 shallow patty tin holes. Using an 8 cm (3¼ inch) cutter, cut out 24 rounds from the pastry sheets. Line the tins with the rounds.

Divide the onion among the pastry cases, then spoon the feta over the onion. Combine the eggs with the cream, season with salt and ground black pepper and pour into the pastry cases. Bake for 10–15 minutes, or until puffed and golden. Leave to cool in the tins for 5 minutes before transferring to a wire rack to cool.

Makes 24

cherry tomato and bocconcini tartlets

apricot and cardamom slice

95 g (3¹/2 oz/¹/2 cup) finely
    chopped dried apricots
100 g (3¹/2 oz) unsalted butter
1 tablespoon honey
2 eggs
115 g (4¹/2 oz/¹/2 cup) caster
    (superfine) sugar
90 g (3¹/4 oz/³/4 cup) self-raising
    flour, sifted

35 g (1¹/4 oz/¹/3 cup) ground
    almonds
1 teaspoon ground cardamom
2 tablespoons caster (superfine)
    sugar, extra
¹/2 teaspoon ground cardamom,
    extra

Preheat the oven to 180°C (350°F/Gas 4). Lightly grease an 18 x 27 cm (7 x 10³/4 inch) shallow baking tin and line the base and sides with baking paper, leaving the paper hanging over two opposite sides.

Soak the apricots in boiling water for 2 minutes. Drain very well. Put the butter and honey in a saucepan over low heat until melted. Cool slightly.

Beat the eggs and sugar with electric beaters until light and fluffy. Fold in the butter and honey, then the flour, almonds, cardamom and apricots. Spread the mixture evenly into the tin. Sprinkle the combined extra sugar and cardamom over the top. Bake for 20 minutes. Cool completely in the tin, then cut into slices to serve.

Makes 18 pieces

peach and almond strudels

225 g (8 oz) tinned sliced
    pie peaches
30 g (1 oz/¼ cup) slivered
    almonds
30 g (1 oz/¼ cup) sultanas

2 teaspoons soft brown sugar
6 sheets filo pastry
30 g (1 oz) butter, melted
ground cinnamon, for dusting

Preheat the oven to 180°C (350°F/Gas 4). Grease 12 x 80 ml (2¹/₂ fl oz/¹/₃ cup) muffin holes.

Mix together the peaches, slivered almonds, sultanas and brown sugar.

Brush a sheet of filo pastry with melted butter, then top with another sheet. Cut into four and cut each piece into four again (16 squares). Repeat with the remaining four sheets of filo to give 48 squares in total. Press four squares into each muffin hole in a star pattern and bake for 10 minutes.

Put 1 tablespoon of filling in each pastry case, dust with cinnamon and bake for 5–10 minutes, or until the pastry is golden.

Makes 12

Bursting with the deep, complex sweetness of cherries, these mini tarts are terribly moreish and as pretty as a picture.

mini cherry galettes

670 g (1 lb 8 oz) jar pitted morello cherries, drained
30 g (1 oz) unsalted butter, softened
1^1/$_2$ tablespoons caster (superfine) sugar
1 egg yolk
^{1}/$_2$ teaspoon vanilla essence
55 g (2 oz/^{1}/$_2$ cup) ground almonds
1 tablespoon plain (all-purpose) flour
2 sheets ready-rolled puff pastry
160 g (5^3/$_4$ oz/^{1}/$_2$ cup) cherry jam

Preheat the oven to 180°C (350°F/Gas 4). Line a baking tray with baking paper. Spread the cherries onto paper towels to absorb any excess liquid.

Combine the butter and sugar in a bowl and beat until creamy. Add the egg yolk and vanilla essence, then stir in the combined almonds and flour. Refrigerate until required.

Cut 30 rounds and ovals from the pastry sheets using a 5 cm (2 inch) round and 6 cm (2¹/₂ inch) oval cutter. Put half the rounds and ovals on the prepared tray and lightly prick them all over with a fork. Cover with another sheet of baking paper and weigh down with another baking tray (this prevents the pastry from rising during cooking). Cook for 10 minutes, remove from the oven and allow to cool on the trays. Repeat with the remaining rounds and ovals. Leave the oven on.

Put 1 level teaspoon of almond mixture in the centre of each cooled pastry and press it flat to a thickness of 3 mm (¹/₈ inch). Press three cherries onto the almond mixture.

Bake for another 8 minutes, or until lightly browned. Put the jam in a cup, stand in a saucepan of hot water and stir until melted. Strain. Use the jam to brush the cherries with a light glaze.

Makes 30

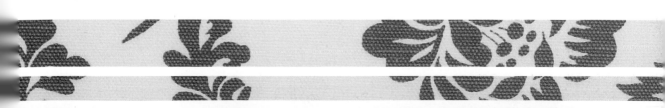

mini cherry galettes

mini lime meringue pies

4 sheets ready-rolled sweet
　　shortcrust pastry
115 g (4 oz/1/2 cup) caster
　　(superfine) sugar
30 g (1 oz/1/4 cup) cornflour
　　(cornstarch)
2 teaspoons grated lime zest

4 tablespoons lime juice
30 g (1 oz) butter
2 egg yolks
3 egg whites
115 g (4 oz/1/2 cup) caster
　　(superfine) sugar, extra

Preheat the oven to 180°C (350°F/Gas 4). Grease two shallow 12-hole patty tins. Using a 7 cm (2³/4 inch) cutter, cut 24 rounds from the pastry sheets. Put the rounds in the tins and prick the bases well with a fork. Bake for 12–15 minutes, or until golden brown, then cool.

Put the sugar, cornflour, lime zest, lime juice and 185 ml (6 fl oz/³/4 cup) of water in a large saucepan. Stir over medium heat until the mixture boils and thickens. Remove from the heat and add the butter. Mix well, then gradually stir in the egg yolks. Spoon 1 heaped teaspoon of the mixture into each pastry case.

Beat the egg whites with electric beaters until stiff peaks form. Gradually add the extra sugar and beat until it dissolves and the mixture is glossy. Spoon 1 tablespoon over each pie. Bake for 4–5 minutes, or until golden.

Makes 24

amaretti

1 tablespoon plain (all-purpose) flour
1 tablespoon cornflour (cornstarch)
1 teaspoon ground cinnamon
145 g (5¼ oz/⅔ cup) caster (superfine) sugar
1 teaspoon grated lemon zest
185 g (6½ oz/1 cup) ground almonds
2 egg whites
30 g (1 oz/¼ cup) icing (confectioners') sugar
candied lemon zest, to serve

Line two baking trays with baking paper. Sift the flours, cinnamon and half the caster sugar into a large bowl. Add the lemon zest and almonds.

Put the egg whites in a small, dry bowl. Beat with electric beaters until soft peaks form. Add the remaining caster sugar gradually, beating constantly until the mixture is thick and glossy and all the sugar has dissolved. Fold into the dry ingredients using a metal spoon. Stir until the mixture is just combined and forms a soft dough. With oiled or wet hands, roll 2 level teaspoons of mixture at a time into a ball. Arrange on the baking trays, allowing room for spreading. Set aside, uncovered, for 1 hour.

Preheat the oven to 180°C (350°F/Gas 4). Sift the icing sugar liberally over the biscuits. Bake for 15–20 minutes, or until crisp and lightly browned. Transfer to a wire rack to cool. Top with candied lemon zest and serve.

Makes 24

Ruby red raspberries bring their deep, rich sweetness to these deliciously chewy slices.

raspberry and coconut slice

280 g (10 oz/2¼ cups) plain (all-purpose) flour
3 tablespoons ground almonds
460 g (1 lb/2 cups) caster (superfine) sugar
250 g (9 oz) unsalted butter, chilled
½ teaspoon ground nutmeg
½ teaspoon baking powder
4 eggs
1 teaspoon vanilla essence
1 tablespoon lemon juice
310 g (11 oz/2½ cups) fresh or thawed frozen raspberries
90 g (3¼ oz/1 cup) desiccated coconut
icing (confectioners') sugar, for dusting

Preheat the oven to 180°C (350°F/Gas 4). Lightly grease a 20 x 30 cm (8 x 12 inch) shallow tin and line with baking paper, hanging over the two long sides.

Sift 215 g (7^1/$_2$ oz/1^3/$_4$ cups) of the flour into a bowl. Add the almonds and 115 g (4 oz/^{1}/$_2$ cup) of sugar and stir to combine. Rub the butter into the flour with your fingertips until it resembles fine breadcrumbs. Press the mixture into the tin and bake for 20–25 minutes, or until golden. Reduce the oven temperature to 150°C (300°F/Gas 2).

Sift the nutmeg, baking powder and the remaining flour onto a piece of baking paper. Beat the eggs, vanilla and remaining sugar with electric beaters for 4 minutes, or until light and fluffy. Fold in the flour with a large metal spoon. Stir in the lemon juice, raspberries and coconut and pour over the base.

Bake for 1 hour, or until golden and firm. Chill in the tin, then cut into pieces. Dust with icing sugar and serve.

Makes 18 pieces

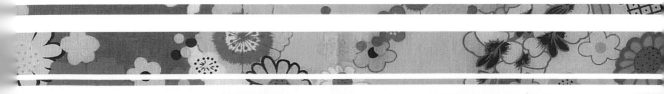

mini lime meringue pies

amaretti

pecan shortbread

50 g (1³/4 oz/¹/2 cup) pecans
125 g (4¹/2 oz) unsalted butter,
    softened
3 tablespoons caster (superfine)
    sugar

90 g (3¹/4 oz/³/4 cup) plain
    (all-purpose) flour, sifted
¹/2 teaspoon vanilla essence
24 pecans, extra

Preheat the oven to 180°C (350°F/Gas 4). Process the pecans in a food processor until finely ground.

In a bowl, beat the butter and caster sugar until light and fluffy. Fold in the flour, vanilla essence and the ground pecans.

Roll 2 teaspoons of the mixture into a ball and flatten onto a baking tray. Gently press one pecan on top and repeat with the remaining mixture to make 24 shortbreads. Bake for 15 minutes, then leave to cool before removing from the baking tray.

Makes 24

chocolate truffle macaroon slice

3 egg whites
170 g (6 oz/3/4 cup) caster
    (superfine) sugar
180 g (6 1/4 oz/2 cups)
    desiccated coconut

250 g (9 oz) good-quality dark
    chocolate, chopped into
    small even-sized pieces
300 ml (10 1/2 fl oz) cream
1 tablespoon cocoa powder

Preheat the oven to 180°C (350°F/Gas 4). Lightly grease a 20 x 30 cm (8 x 12 inch) shallow baking tin and line with baking paper, leaving it hanging over the two long sides.

Beat the egg whites in a clean, dry bowl until soft peaks form. Slowly add the sugar, beating well after each addition, until stiff and glossy. Fold in the coconut. Spread into the tin. Bake for 20 minutes, or until light brown. While still warm, press down lightly but firmly with a palette knife. Cool completely.

Put the chocolate in a heatproof bowl. Bring a saucepan of water to the boil, then remove from the heat. Sit the bowl over the pan, making sure the bowl doesn't touch the water. Leave, stirring occasionally, until the chocolate has melted. Cool slightly. Beat the cream until thick. Gently fold in the chocolate — don't overmix or it will curdle. Spread the chocolate cream evenly over the coconut base and refrigerate for 3 hours, or until set. Lift from the tin and dust with the cocoa.

Makes 24 pieces

mini mud cakes

170 g (6 oz/³/4 cup) caster (superfine) sugar
175 g (6 oz) good-quality dark chocolate, chopped
90 g (3¹/4 oz) unsalted butter, chopped
2 eggs, lightly beaten
2 tablespoons brandy
60 g (2¹/4 oz/¹/2 cup) plain (all-purpose) flour
60 g (2¹/4 oz/¹/2 cup) self-raising flour
30 g (1 oz/¹/4 cup) cocoa powder
50 g (1³/4 oz/¹/3 cup) milk chocolate melts (buttons)
200 g (7 oz/1¹/3 cups) dark chocolate melts (buttons), chopped
125 ml (4 fl oz/¹/2 cup) cream

Preheat the oven to 180°C (350°F/Gas 4). Grease the base and sides of a 20 x 30 cm (8 x 12 inch) baking tin. Cover the base and two long sides with baking paper. Put the sugar, chocolate, butter and 3 tablespoons of water in a saucepan and stir over low heat for 5 minutes, or until melted. Cool to room temperature, then stir in the eggs and brandy.

Sift the flours and cocoa into a bowl and make a well in the centre. Pour in the chocolate mixture, stir well and pour into the tin. Bake for about 20–25 minutes, or until a skewer inserted into the centre comes out clean. Cool in the tin for 5 minutes, then invert onto a wire cake rack to cool.

Dip a 3 cm (1 1/4 inch) round cutter in hot water and cut out 30 rounds of cake, re-dipping the cutter each time (this makes a neater edge). Roll the cut surface gently on the bench to press in any crumbs. Arrange the cakes, top-side down, on a wire cake rack over an oven tray.

Put the milk chocolate melts in a heatproof bowl. Bring a saucepan of water to the boil, then remove from the heat. Sit the bowl over the pan, stirring occasionally, until the chocolate has melted. Spread the chocolate fairly thinly over a marble board or cool baking tray and leave until just set. Using the edge of a sharp knife at a 45 degree angle, scrape over the top of the chocolate. The strips will curl as they come away. If the chocolate has set too firmly, the curls will break. Leave in a warm place and try again.

Put the dark chocolate melts in a bowl. Heat the cream until almost boiling and pour over the chocolate. Leave for 2 minutes, then stir until the chocolate melts and is smooth. Spoon the chocolate mixture evenly over the cakes, reheating gently if the mixture becomes too thick. Tap the tray gently to settle the chocolate, top each cake with a chocolate curl and leave to set. Use a palette knife to remove from the cake rack.

Makes 30

pecan shortbread

baby florentines

90 g (3¹/4 oz) butter
115 g (4 oz/¹/2 cup) caster
   (superfine) sugar
1 tablespoon honey
45 g (1¹/2 oz/heaped ¹/3 cup)
   slivered almonds, chopped
45 g (1³/4 oz) mixed peel

60 g (2¹/4 oz/¹/3 cup) dried
   apricots, finely chopped
2 tablespoons chopped glacé
   cherries
60 g (2¹/4 oz/¹/2 cup) plain
   (all-purpose) flour
150 g (5¹/2 oz) dark chocolate

Preheat the oven to 180°C (350°F/Gas 4). Cover two baking trays with baking paper. Melt the butter, sugar and honey in a saucepan. Remove from the heat and stir in the almonds, fruit and the flour. Roll teaspoons of the mixture into balls and arrange on the trays, allowing room for spreading. Press lightly with your fingertips into 3 cm (1¹/4 inch) rounds.

Bake for 8–10 minutes, or until golden. Cool on the trays until slightly firm. Using a spatula, carefully remove and cool completely on wire racks.

Bring a saucepan of water to the boil and remove from the heat. Put the chocolate in a heatproof bowl and sit the bowl over the pan, making sure the bowl does not touch the water. Stir occasionally until the chocolate has melted. Spread a thin layer of chocolate quickly over the backs of the florentines, then leave to set, chocolate-side-up.

Makes about 50

orange and almond friands

165 g (5³/4 oz/1¹/3 cups) icing
    (confectioners') sugar
50 g (1³/4 oz/heaped ¹/3 cup)
    plain (all-purpose) flour
100 g (3¹/2 oz/1 cup) ground
    almonds
3 egg whites
150 g (5¹/2 oz) butter, melted
    and strained

2 teaspoons orange zest
¹/4 teaspoon orange flower
    water
icing (confectioners') sugar,
    extra, for dusting
Persian fairy floss and orange
    zest, to garnish (optional)

Preheat the oven to 180°C (350°F/Gas 4). Grease 30 x 20 ml (¹/2 fl oz) mini cake tins. Sift the icing sugar and flour into a bowl, add the ground almonds and mix well.

Beat the egg whites until soft peaks form and fold into the mixture. Add the butter, orange zest and orange flower water and stir well.

Spoon the mixture into the tins and bake for 8 minutes. Remove and cool slightly before removing from the tray and dusting with icing sugar. Garnish with a swirl of Persian fairy floss (available from Middle Eastern food stores) and some orange zest.

Makes 30

Devilishly good and strikingly elegant, these finger-sized morsels bring a touch of Gallic glamour to a thoroughly English repast.

mini éclairs

60 g (2¼ oz) unsalted butter, chopped
125 g (4½ oz/1 cup) plain (all-purpose) flour, sifted
4 eggs, beaten

300 ml (10½ fl oz) cream
1 tablespoon icing (confectioners') sugar, sifted
½ teaspoon vanilla essence
50 g (1¾ oz) dark chocolate

Preheat the oven to 200°C (400°F/Gas 6) and line two baking trays with baking paper. Put the butter in a small saucepan with 250 ml (9 fl oz/ 1 cup) of water and stir over low heat until melted. Bring to the boil, then immediately remove from the heat and add the flour all at once. Beat with a wooden spoon until smooth. Return to the heat and beat for 2 minutes, or until the mixture forms a ball and leaves the sides of the pan. Remove from the heat and transfer to a bowl. Cool for 5 minutes. Add the egg, a little at a time, beating well after each addition, until thick and glossy — a wooden spoon should stand upright in the mixture.

Spoon the mixture into a piping bag with a 1.2 cm ($^1/_2$ inch) plain nozzle (you may need to do this in batches). Pipe 6 cm ($2^1/_2$ inch) lengths of batter onto the baking trays. Bake for 10 minutes, then reduce the heat to 180°C (350°F/Gas 4) and cook for 10 minutes, or until golden and puffed. Split the éclairs and remove the soft dough from the middle. Return to the oven for another 2–3 minutes to dry out a little more. Cool on a wire rack.

Put the cream, icing sugar and vanilla in a bowl and whip until thick. Spoon into a piping bag and pipe into the bottom of each éclair. Replace the éclair pastry tops.

Put the chocolate in a heatproof bowl. Bring a saucepan of water to the boil, then remove the pan from the heat. Sit the bowl over the pan, making sure the bowl does not touch the water. Stir occasionally until melted.

Spoon the chocolate into a small plastic bag and push into a corner. Snip a small hole in the corner and drizzle stripes over each éclair.

Makes 24

orange and almond friands

high heels and cocktails Hit the cocktail hour and the party really starts. When the dresses are slinkier and the liquor harder, the food needs to edge up a notch or more. Forget about keeping

it simple, this is your chance to go all out and show what you can do. Be creative, be adventurous because there's no such thing as over the top when it comes to the true home of the canapé.

Weddings, birthdays, anniversaries — any event that demands proper celebration is the perfect excuse, should you need one, to throw a cocktail party. As the name suggests, at a cocktail party the food and drinks are of equal importance and it's the equal part that's paramount. The biggest, and most common, mistake made at cocktail parties is when the drinks are prioritized at the expense of the food. Unless you want things to get really messy it's wise to make sure there is plenty of food to go around. If your guests have to pounce on the trays, the food isn't coming out quick enough and if the room starts spinning, it's not substantial enough. Make sure there's a good mix of light food and some dishes with substance. It's also important to cater to all tastes and preferences with an inventive mix of spicy and non-spicy, seafood, meat and vegetarian. Of all possible events, cocktail parties require the most planning, the largest investment and the biggest army of helpers, but the result, when you pull it off, is its own reward. Recruit some friends to help decorate, prepare, cook and serve so you have time to mingle. You might like to delegate the creation of cocktails to a couple of experienced mixologists, amateur or otherwise. Leave yourself a little bit of time to change and freshen up, then take a deep breath, get the ball rolling and enjoy a sparkling evening.

219

sesame and wasabi-crusted tuna cubes

ginger soy dipping sauce
2 x 2 cm (3/4 x 3/4 inch) piece
    of fresh ginger, cut into
    julienne strips
2 tablespoons Japanese
    soy sauce
2 tablespoons mirin
1 teaspoon wasabi paste
1/4 teaspoon sesame oil

600 g (1 lb 5 oz) fresh tuna
    steaks, cut into 2 cm
    (3/4 inch) cubes
1 teaspoon wasabi powder
50 g (13/4 oz/1/3 cup) black
    sesame seeds
3 tablespoons oil

To make the dipping sauce, combine the ingredients in a small bowl.

Toss the tuna cubes with the combined wasabi powder and black sesame seeds until evenly coated.

Heat a wok over high heat, add half the oil and swirl to coat. Add half the tuna and cook, tossing gently, for 1–2 minutes, or until lightly golden on the outside but still pink in the middle. Drain on crumpled paper towels and repeat with the remaining oil and tuna. Arrange on a platter with the dipping sauce in the centre and serve with toothpicks.

Makes about 40

seared salmon cubes with ginger and almond sauce

ginger and almond sauce
110 g (3½ oz/½ cup) sugar
3 tablespoons white vinegar
3 tablespoons lime juice
1 garlic clove, chopped
1 tablespoon chopped fresh
  ginger
1 tablespoon toasted slivered
  almonds

1 tablespoon chopped coriander
  (cilantro) leaves
1 tablespoon fish sauce

600 g (1 lb 5 oz) salmon fillet
1 tablespoon cracked black
  pepper
1 teaspoon sea salt
2 tablespoons olive oil

To make the sauce, put the sugar, vinegar, lime juice, garlic, ginger and 125 ml (4 fl oz/½ cup) of water in a small saucepan. Stir over low heat until the sugar has dissolved. Simmer for 5–8 minutes, then stir in the almonds, coriander and fish sauce. Set aside until ready to serve.

Remove the skin and bones from the salmon and cut into 2 cm (3/4 inch) cubes. Toss in the combined black pepper and sea salt until evenly coated.

Heat the olive oil in a large frying pan and brown the salmon over high heat. Serve with the ginger and almond sauce and toothpicks.

Makes about 40

Delicate and delicious, these rolls are perfect for the cocktail hour, offering a flawless mouthful without being a handful.

vietnamese rice paper rolls

nuoc cham dipping sauce
185 ml (6 fl oz/3/4 cup) fish sauce
3 tablespoons lime juice
2 tablespoons grated palm sugar or soft brown sugar
2 bird's eye chillies, seeded and finely chopped

150 g (5 1/2 oz) dried rice vermicelli
48 x 15 cm (6 inch) round rice paper wrappers
48 cooked king prawns (shrimp), peeled, deveined
    and halved lengthways
150 g (5 1/2 oz/1 2/3 cups) bean sprouts
3 large handfuls Vietnamese mint
2 large handfuls coriander (cilantro) leaves
2 Lebanese (short) cucumbers, cut in half lengthways,
    seeded and cut into thin strips

To make the dipping sauce, combine all the ingredients and 125 ml (4 fl oz/1/2 cup) of water and stir until the sugar has dissolved. Transfer to a small serving dish and set aside.

Put the noodles in a heatproof bowl, cover with boiling water and soak for 10 minutes. Drain.

Assemble the rolls one at a time. Dip a rice paper wrapper in a bowl of warm water for 30 seconds, or until it softens. Lay the wrapper on a work surface and put two prawn halves on the bottom third of the wrapper. Top with a few noodles, bean sprouts, three mint leaves, six coriander leaves and a cucumber strip, in that order. Ensure that the filling is neat and compact, then turn up the bottom of the wrapper to cover the filling. Holding the filling in place, fold in the two sides, then roll up.

Arrange on a platter, folded-side-down. Cover with a damp tea towel or plastic wrap until ready to serve. Serve with the dipping sauce.

Makes 48

vietnamese rice paper rolls

basic sushi rice

550 g (1 lb 4 oz/2¹/₂ cups) sushi rice (such as Japonica rice, available from Asian food stores)

dressing
100 ml (3¹/₂ fl oz) rice vinegar
2 tablespoons sugar
1 tablespoon mirin

Rinse the rice under cold running water until the water runs clear, then sit it in a strainer for 1 hour to drain. Put the rice in a large saucepan with 750 ml (26 fl oz/3 cups) of water. Bring to the boil and cook, without stirring, for 5–10 minutes, or until tunnels start to form on the surface. Reduce the heat to low and cook, covered, for 12–15 minutes, or until tender. Remove from the heat, take off the lid and cover with a clean tea towel. Leave for 15 minutes.

To make the dressing, combine the vinegar, sugar, mirin and 1 teaspoon of salt in a bowl and stir until the sugar has dissolved.

Spread the rice over a flat, non-metallic tray, pour the dressing on top and mix with a spatula. Gently separate the grains of rice. Spread out the rice and cool to body temperature — if it gets too cold, it will turn hard and be difficult to work with. Spread a damp tea towel over the rice and keep it covered as you work. To prevent rice from sticking to your hands, dip them in a bowl of warm water mixed with a few drops of rice vinegar.

Makes about 1.1 kg (2 lb 8 oz/6 cups)

nigiri zushi

250 g (9 oz) sashimi tuna
    or salmon
juice of 1 lemon
1.1 kg (2 lb 8 oz/6 cups)
    prepared sushi rice
    (see facing page)

2 teaspoons wasabi paste
1 sheet of nori, cut into strips

Use a sharp knife to trim the fish into a neat rectangle, then cut into paper-thin slices, cleaning your knife in a bowl of water mixed with the lemon juice after cutting each slice.

Form 1 tablespoon of sushi rice into an oval about the same size as your pieces of fish. Put a piece of fish on the open palm of your left hand, then spread a small dab of wasabi over the centre. Put the rice on the fish and gently cup your palm to make a curve. Using the middle and index fingers of your right hand, press the rice onto the fish, firmly pushing with a slight downward motion to make a neat shape. Turn over and repeat the shaping process, finishing with the fish on top of the rice. Tie a nori strip around the centre. Repeat with the remaining ingredients.

Makes 16–20

To make these little rolls, splurge on the freshest tuna you can find and spice it up with the heat of the best Japanese wasabi.

maki zushi

8 sheets of nori
550 g (1 lb 4 oz/3 cups) prepared sushi rice
   (see page 226)
3 teaspoons wasabi paste
250 g (9 oz) sashimi tuna, cut into thin strips
1 small Lebanese (short) cucumber, cut into thin strips
1/2 avocado, cut into thin strips

Put a sheet of nori on a bamboo sushi mat, shiny-side-down, with a short end towards you. (Bamboo sushi mats are available at Asian grocery stores; there isn't really a substitute if you want to make successful sushi.) Spread the rice about 1 cm (1/2 inch) thick over the nori, leaving a 1 cm (1/2 inch) border.

Make a shallow groove across the rice towards the short end closest to you. Spread a small amount of wasabi along the groove. Arrange some of the tuna, cucumber and avocado strips on top of the wasabi. Lift up the edge of the bamboo mat and roll the sushi, starting from the edge nearest to you. When you've finished rolling, press the mat to make either a round or square roll. Push in any rice that is escaping from the ends. Wet a sharp knife, trim the ends and cut the roll in half and then each half into three pieces. Repeat with the remaining ingredients.

Makes 48

maki zushi

asian crab tarts

3 tablespoons lime juice
1 tablespoon fish sauce
1 tablespoon grated palm sugar
or soft brown sugar
300 g (10½ oz) fresh crab meat,
shredded and well drained
2 tablespoons chopped
coriander (cilantro) leaves
1 tablespoon chopped
Vietnamese mint

1 small red chilli, seeded
and finely chopped
2 makrut (kaffir lime) leaves,
finely shredded
24 cooked tartlet cases
(see page 186)
24 small Vietnamese mint
leaves

Combine the lime juice, fish sauce and sugar in a bowl and stir until the sugar has dissolved.

Add the crab meat, coriander, mint, chilli and shredded lime leaves and mix together well. Spoon the filling into the tartlet cases and garnish with the Vietnamese mint leaves.

Makes 24

wasabi crème fraîche oysters

24 fresh oysters on the half shell
80 ml (2^1/$_2$ fl oz/^{1}/$_3$ cup) crème
   fraîche
2 tablespoons whole-egg
   mayonnaise

1^1/$_2$ teaspoons wasabi paste
flying fish or fish roe, to garnish
small lime wedges, to garnish

Remove the oysters from their shells. Wash the shells with hot water and pat dry. Replace the oysters and cover them with a damp cloth in the refrigerator.

Put the crème fraîche, mayonnaise and wasabi paste in a bowl and whisk until well combined.

Put a teaspoon of the mixture on top of each oyster, then garnish with the roe and lime wedges.

Makes 24

vegetable dumplings

8 dried Chinese mushrooms
1 tablespoon oil
2 teaspoons finely chopped fresh ginger
2 garlic cloves, crushed
100 g (3^1/$_2$ oz) Chinese chives, chopped
100 g (3^1/$_2$ oz) water spinach, cut into 1 cm (^{1}/$_2$ inch) lengths
3 tablespoons chicken stock
2 tablespoons oyster sauce
1 tablespoon cornflour (cornstarch)
1 teaspoon soy sauce
1 teaspoon rice wine
45 g (1^1/$_2$ oz/^{1}/$_4$ cup) chopped water chestnuts

wrappers
200 g (7 oz/1^2/$_3$ cups) wheat starch
1 teaspoon cornflour (cornstarch)
oil, for kneading

Soak the mushrooms in 500 ml (17 fl oz/2 cups) of hot water for about
15 minutes. Discard the stems and finely chop the caps.

Heat the oil in a frying pan over high heat and cook the ginger and garlic for 30 seconds. Add the chives and water spinach and cook for 1 minute.

Combine the stock, oyster sauce, cornflour, soy sauce and rice wine and add to the spinach mixture. Stir in the water chestnuts and mushrooms. Cook for 1–2 minutes, or until the mixture thickens. Cool completely.

To make the wrappers, combine the wheat starch and cornflour in a bowl. Make a well in the centre and add 185 ml (6 fl oz/$3/4$ cup) of boiling water, a little at a time, bringing the mixture together with your hands. Knead it immediately with lightly oiled hands until the dough forms a shiny ball.

Keep the dough covered with a cloth while you work. Pick walnut-sized pieces of dough and, using well-oiled hands, squash them between the palms of your hands then roll out as thinly as possible into 10 cm (4 inch) circles. Put 1 tablespoon of the filling in the centre of the circle. Pinch the edges of the wrapper together to enclose the filling and form a tight ball.

Fill a wok one-third full of water and bring to the boil. Put the dumplings in a bamboo steamer lined with baking paper, leaving a gap between each one. Cover and steam for 7–8 minutes. Delicious with chilli sauce.

Makes 24

asian crab tarts

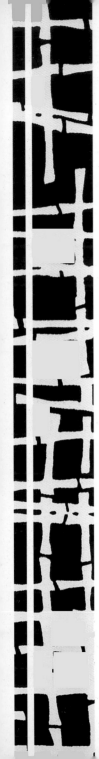

tomato, chilli and coriander oysters

24 fresh oysters on the half shell
2 vine-ripened tomatoes,
    seeded and finely diced
2 French shallots, finely
    chopped
2 small red chillies, seeded
    and sliced

3 tablespoons chopped
    coriander (cilantro) leaves
1 tablespoon lime juice
lime wedges, to serve

Remove the oysters from their shells. Wash the shells in hot water, then pat dry. Replace the oysters and cover with a damp cloth in the refrigerator.

Put the tomato, shallots, chilli and coriander in a bowl and mix together well. Stir in the lime juice, then season to taste with salt and pepper. Put a teaspoon of salsa on each oyster. Serve with lime wedges for extra juice.

Makes 24

oysters with prosciutto and balsamic vinegar

24 fresh oysters on the half shell
2–3 tablespoons balsamic
    vinegar
6 slices prosciutto, each
    chopped into 4 thin strips

Remove the oysters from their shells. Wash the shells in hot water and
pat dry. Replace the oysters and put them on a baking tray. Drizzle the
balsamic vinegar over the oysters and arrange a coil of prosciutto on top.
Season with cracked black pepper.

Cook under a hot grill (broiler) for about 1 minute, or until the prosciutto
is starting to crisp.

Makes 24

Cocktails bring on cravings for crispy, salty tidbits — a platter of these will scratch the itch without lowering the tone.

won ton stacks with tuna and ginger

12 fresh won ton wrappers
125 ml (4 fl oz/^{1}/$_2$ cup) peanut or
    vegetable oil
60 g (2^1/$_4$ oz/^{1}/$_4$ cup) Japanese mayonnaise
150 g (5^1/$_2$ oz) piece of fresh tuna fillet
    (such as sashimi tuna), cut into 24 thin slices
50 g (1^3/$_4$ oz) pickled ginger
50 g (1^3/$_4$ oz) snowpea sprouts
1^1/$_2$ tablespoons sesame seeds, toasted
2 teaspoons mirin
2 teaspoons soy sauce
^{1}/$_4$ teaspoon sugar

Cut the won ton wrappers into quarters to give 48 squares in total. Heat the oil in a small saucepan over medium heat and cook the wrappers in batches for 1–2 minutes, or until they are golden and crisp. Drain on crumpled paper towels.

Spoon ¼ teaspoon of the mayonnaise onto 24 of the won ton squares. Put a slice of tuna on the mayonnaise and top with a little of the pickled ginger, snowpea sprouts and sesame seeds.

Mix the mirin, soy sauce and sugar together in a small bowl and drizzle a little over each stack. Season with pepper. Top with the remaining 24 won ton squares. Serve immediately or the stacks will become soggy.

Makes 24

tomato, chilli and coriander oysters

oysters with prosciutto and
balsamic vinegar

scallops with lime hollandaise sauce

1 egg yolk
1 tablespoon lime juice
45 g (1 1/2 oz) butter, melted

1 tablespoon snipped chives
24 scallops on the half shell

Mix the egg yolk and lime juice in a food processor for 30 seconds. With the motor running, add the melted butter in a thin stream. Transfer to a bowl, add the chives and season with salt and pepper.

Preheat the oven to 180°C (350°F/Gas 4). Using a sharp knife, carefully cut the scallops from their shells, as cleanly as possible, and remove the vein and white muscle. Wash the shells in hot water and warm through on a baking tray in the oven for 5 minutes.

Cook the scallops in a chargrill pan (griddle) or frying pan over high heat for about 1 minute each side, then return them to their shells. Spoon 1 teaspoon of the lime hollandaise over each scallop and serve.

Makes 24

oysters with tarragon vinaigrette

24 fresh oysters on the half shell
1 tablespoon chopped tarragon
1 small spring onion (scallion),
   finely chopped

2 teaspoons white wine vinegar
1 tablespoon lemon juice
2 tablespoons extra virgin
   olive oil

Remove the oysters from their shells. Wash the shells in hot water and set aside. Combine the oysters with the tarragon, spring onion, vinegar, lemon juice and olive oil, then cover and refrigerate for 30 minutes.

Arrange the oyster shells on a serving plate and spoon an oyster back into each shell. Drizzle with any remaining vinaigrette and serve.

Makes 24

Sesame oil in the pancake dough lends a subtle, nutty taste that brings out the flavour yet cuts through the richness of the duck.

peking duck rolls

125 g (4¹/2 oz/1 cup) plain (all-purpose) flour
¹/2 teaspoon sesame oil
¹/2 large Chinese roast duck
6 spring onions (scallions), cut into 6 cm (2¹/2 inch) lengths (24 pieces in total)

1 Lebanese (short) cucumber, seeded and cut into 6 cm x 5 mm (2¹/2 x ¹/4 inch) batons
2–3 tablespoons hoisin sauce
2 teaspoons sesame seeds, toasted
24 chives, blanched

Sift the flour into a small bowl, make a well in the centre and pour in the sesame oil and 125 ml (4 fl oz/¹/2 cup) of boiling water. Mix well until it forms a slightly sticky soft dough (add a few more teaspoons of boiling water if the mixture is still a bit dry). Knead the dough on a floured work surface for 5 minutes, or until smooth. Cover and rest for 10 minutes.

Shred the duck meat into pieces with your fingers and cut the skin into small strips.

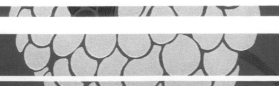

Roll the dough into a sausage shape and divide into 24 pieces. On a lightly floured board, roll each piece to an 8–9 cm (3^1/$_4$–3^1/$_2$ inch) round with a rolling pin. Once they are rolled out, lay out the rounds in a single layer and cover with plastic wrap or a clean tea towel while you are making the others to prevent them from drying out.

Heat a non-stick frying pan over medium heat and dry-fry the pancakes in batches for about 20 seconds on each side. Do not overcook, or they will become too crispy for rolling. The pancakes should have slight brown speckles on them. Stack each pancake on a plate, and keep warm. If they cool down too much, wrap them in foil and reheat in a warm (170°C/325°F/Gas 3) oven or microwave for 20–30 seconds on high.

Arrange a piece of spring onion, cucumber, duck flesh and skin on each pancake. Drizzle with ^{1}/$_2$ teaspoon of hoisin sauce and sprinkle with sesame seeds. Roll up firmly and tie each pancake with a blanched chive.

Makes 24

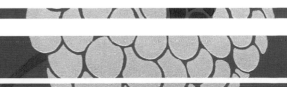

peking duck rolls

oysters with ginger and shallots

24 fresh oysters on the half shell
2 tablespoons Japanese
   soy sauce
1 tablespoon mirin
2 teaspoons sake
1/2 teaspoon sugar

1 1/2 tablespoons thinly sliced
   fresh ginger
2 tablespoons thinly sliced
   spring onion (scallion)
2 teaspoons sesame oil
toasted sesame seeds, to garnish

Remove the oysters from their shells. Wash the shells in hot water and pat dry. Replace the oysters and cover with a damp cloth in the refrigerator.

Put the soy sauce, mirin, sake and sugar in a small saucepan and mix together well. Simmer over low heat, stirring, until the sugar dissolves, then add the ginger and spring onion. Simmer for 1 minute, then stir in the sesame oil.

Spoon about 1/2 teaspoon of the sauce over each oyster. Sprinkle with sesame seeds and serve.

Makes 24

oysters and lemon herb dressing

24 fresh oysters on the half shell
1 tablespoon chopped dill
1 garlic clove, crushed
1 tablespoon finely chopped
    flat-leaf (Italian) parsley
2 teaspoons finely chopped
    chives

2 tablespoons lemon juice
3 tablespoons extra virgin
    olive oil
brown bread, cut into small
    cubes, to serve

Remove the oysters from their shells. Wash the shells in hot water and pat dry. Replace the oysters and cover with a damp cloth in the refrigerator.

Put the dill, garlic, parsley, chives, lemon juice and oil in a bowl and season to taste with salt and cracked black pepper. Mix together well.

Drizzle a little of the dressing over each oyster and serve with the cubes of brown bread.

Makes 24

Part of an elegant and elaborate eating experience, the noodles add an extra crunch and soak up the tangy dipping sauce.

prawn, noodle and nori parcels

250 g (9 oz) dried somen
   noodles
3 sheets of nori
60 g (2¹/4 oz/¹/2 cup) plain
   (all-purpose) flour
2 egg yolks
24 raw prawns (shrimp),
   peeled and deveined,
   tails intact
oil, for deep-frying

dipping sauce
4 tablespoons tonkatsu sauce
   or barbecue sauce
2 tablespoons lemon juice
1 tablespoon sake or mirin
1–2 teaspoons grated fresh
   ginger, to taste

To make the dipping sauce, combine all the ingredients in a small bowl.

Using a sharp knife, cut the noodles to the same length as the prawn bodies (from the head to the base of the tail). Keep the noodles in neat bundles and set aside. Cut the nori into 2.5 cm (1 inch) wide strips.

Sift the flour into a large bowl and make a well in the centre. Mix the egg yolks with 3 tablespoons of water. Gradually add to the flour, whisking to make a smooth lump-free batter. Add another tablespoon of water if the mixture is too thick.

Dip a prawn in the batter, letting the excess run off. Roll the prawn lengthways in noodles to coat it with a single layer. Keep the noodles in place by rolling a nori strip around the centre of the prawn and securing it with a little batter. Repeat with the rest of the prawns.

Fill a deep heavy-based saucepan one-third full of oil and heat to 180°C (350°F), or until a cube of bread dropped in the oil browns in 15 seconds. Deep-fry 2–3 prawns at a time for 1 minute, or until the prawns are cooked. Drain on crumpled paper towels and keep warm while cooking the rest. Serve warm with the dipping sauce.

Makes 24

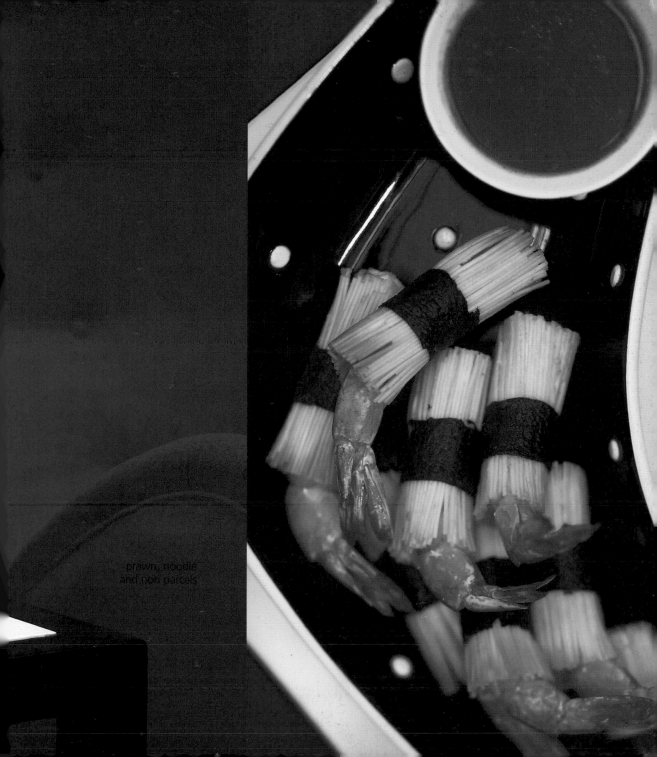

prawn, noodle
and nori parcels

fresh herb pakoras

165 g (5³/4 oz/1¹/2 cups) besan
    (chickpea) flour
1 teaspoon ground turmeric
1/2 teaspoon chilli powder
1¹/2 teaspoons garam masala
1 zucchini (courgette), diced
1 small orange sweet potato,
    diced
60 g (2¹/4 oz) cauliflower florets
50 g (1³/4 oz/¹/3 cup) frozen
    peas, thawed

1 small onion, diced
2 tablespoons chopped
    coriander (cilantro) leaves
2 tablespoons chopped basil
2 tablespoons chopped parsley
2 garlic cloves, crushed
oil, for deep-frying
plain yoghurt and mango
    chutney, to serve

Sift the flour, turmeric, chilli powder, garam masala and 1¹/2 teaspoons of salt into a bowl. Make a well and gradually add 125 ml (4 fl oz/¹/2 cup) of water, whisking to a stiff lump-free batter. Cover and leave for 30 minutes.

Beat the mixture again and stir in the vegetables, herbs and garlic.

Fill a deep heavy-based saucepan one-third full of oil and heat to 180°C (350°F), or until a cube of bread browns in 15 seconds. Drop heaped teaspoons of mixture into the oil in batches and cook until golden. Drain on paper towels. Serve with yoghurt and mango chutney for dipping.

Makes 30

tandoori prawns

125 g (4¹/₂ oz/¹/₂ cup) plain
   yoghurt
1 very large handful coriander
   (cilantro) leaves, finely
   chopped
2 tablespoons finely chopped
   mint
24 raw king prawns (shrimp),
   peeled and deveined, tails
   intact
2 garlic cloves, crushed

1 tablespoon chopped fresh
   ginger
1 teaspoon chilli powder
1 teaspoon ground turmeric
1 teaspoon ground coriander
1 teaspoon garam masala
a few drops of red food
   colouring (optional)
lemon wedges, to serve

Combine the yoghurt, coriander, mint and some salt, to taste. Pour over the prawns, mix well and leave for 5 minutes.

Mix the garlic, ginger, chilli powder, turmeric, coriander, garam masala and food colouring in a bowl. Add the prawns and marinate for 10 minutes.

Thread the prawns onto metal skewers and barbecue or grill (broil) for 5 minutes. Turn the skewers once, so the prawns cook evenly. They are ready when they start to curl and turn opaque. Serve with lemon wedges.

Makes 24

indian fritters

batter
145 g (5¼ oz/1⅓ cups) besan (chickpea) flour
75 g (2½ oz) rice flour
1 teaspoon ground turmeric
1 teaspoon chilli powder
¼ teaspoon nigella seeds

yoghurt dip
½ Lebanese (short) cucumber, peeled, seeded and
    finely chopped
1 garlic clove, crushed
1 tablespoon chopped mint
125 g (4½ oz/½ cup) plain yoghurt

2 potatoes, peeled and cut into very thin slices
300 g (10½ oz) pumpkin (squash), seeded and cut into
    very thin slices
300 g (10½ oz) eggplant (aubergine), cut into thin slices,
    then halved
15 baby English spinach leaves
oil, for deep-frying
110 g (3¾ oz/1 cup) besan (chickpea) flour

To make the batter, sift the flours, turmeric, chilli powder and $1/2$ teaspoon of salt into a large bowl and make a well in the centre. Gradually add 250 ml (9 fl oz/1 cup) of water, whisking to make a smooth, thick batter. Stir in the nigella seeds, cover and leave for 10 minutes.

To make the dip, combine all the ingredients in a bowl. Refrigerate until ready to serve.

Check the consistency of the batter. It should be like cream so if it is too thick, add another 2–3 tablespoons of water. Half-fill a deep heavy-based saucepan with oil and heat to 180°C (350°F), or until a cube of bread dropped in the oil browns in 15 seconds. Check by cooking $1/4$ teaspoon of batter — if it keeps its shape and sizzles while rising to the top, it is ready. Make sure the oil stays at the same temperature and does not get too hot. The fritters should cook through as well as brown.

259

Dip batches of the vegetables in the besan flour, shake well, then dip in the batter. Deep-fry until golden brown (the cooking time will vary for each vegetable). Drain on crumpled paper towels, sprinkle with salt and keep warm in a slow (150°C/300°F/Gas 2) oven while cooking the remaining batches. Serve immediately with the dip.

Serves 8

indian fritters

mini tortillas with chorizo salsa

4 x 20 cm (8 inch) round flour
   tortillas
2 tablespoons olive oil
250 g (9 oz) chorizo sausages,
   cut into small cubes
90 g (3^1/$_4$ oz/^{1}/$_3$ cup) plain
   yoghurt
1^1/$_2$ large handfuls coriander
   (cilantro), finely chopped

1 ripe avocado, diced
1 large tomato, seeded and
   diced
^{1}/$_4$ red onion, finely chopped
2 teaspoons balsamic vinegar
1 tablespoon virgin olive oil
30 small coriander (cilantro)
   leaves, extra

Preheat the oven to 180°C (350°F/Gas 4). Cut eight circles from each tortilla with a 5.5 cm (2^1/$_4$ inch) cutter, or cut into triangles. Heat 1 tablespoon of oil in a large non-stick frying pan, add one-third of the mini tortillas and cook in a single layer, turning once, until crisp and golden. Drain on paper towels. Repeat with the remaining oil and tortillas.

Put the sausage cubes on a baking tray and bake for 10 minutes, or until cooked through. Drain on crumpled paper towels and leave to cool.

Combine the yoghurt and coriander. Put the avocado, tomato and onion in a bowl, add the sausage, vinegar and oil and season. Stir gently, then spoon onto the tortillas. Top with the yoghurt mixture and coriander.

Makes 32

taco chicken quesadillas

1 tablespoon oil
1 red onion, finely chopped
1 red capsicum (pepper),
    finely diced
2 garlic cloves, crushed
1/4 teaspoon paprika
1 teaspoon ground cumin
1 teaspoon ground coriander
400 g (14 oz) minced (ground)
    chicken

400 g (14 oz) tin chopped
    tomatoes
7 flour tortillas
215 g (7^1/2 oz/1^3/4 cups)
    grated Cheddar cheese
sliced spring onion (scallion),
    to garnish

Preheat the oven to 180°C (350°F/Gas 4). Heat the oil in a large frying pan and cook the onion and capsicum until the onion has softened. Stir in the garlic, paprika, cumin and coriander and cook for about 2 minutes. Add the chicken and cook for 5–8 minutes, or until brown, breaking up any lumps. Stir in the tomato and simmer for 20 minutes, or until thick.

Using an 8 cm (3^1/4 inch) cutter, cut six rounds from each tortilla. Put a teaspoon of the chicken mixture on one half of each round and sprinkle with cheese. Bake for 1 minute, or until the cheese has melted. Fold over and hold for a few seconds to stick. Garnish with spring onion.

Makes 42

Fish and chips with mushy peas is rarely seen as a delicacy, but this modern interpretation will make you seriously reconsider.

scallops on potato crisps with pea purée

20 g (3/4 oz) butter
3 French shallots, finely chopped
1 garlic clove, finely chopped
2 slices mild pancetta, finely chopped
155 g (5 1/2 oz/1 cup) frozen peas
3 tablespoons chicken stock or water
oil, for deep-frying
2–3 floury potatoes (such as russet, King Edward),
    peeled and very thinly sliced to get 24 slices
24 scallops
mint leaves, to garnish

Melt the butter in a saucepan over low heat. Cook the shallots, garlic and pancetta for 3 minutes, or until soft but not coloured. Add the peas and stock. Cook over high heat for 3 minutes, or until the liquid has evaporated. Cool a little, then purée in a food processor until smooth. Season.

Fill a deep heavy-based saucepan one-third full of oil and heat to 190°C (375°F), or until a cube of bread dropped in the oil browns in 10 seconds. Cook the potato slices in batches until crisp and golden. Drain on crumpled paper towels and sprinkle with salt.

Toss the scallops with 1 tablespoon of oil. Season lightly. Heat a chargrill pan (griddle) to hot, then sear the scallops in batches for 5 seconds each side, or until lightly browned on the outside but opaque in the middle. Cut each scallop in half.

Reheat the pea purée. Spread a little on the bottom half of each scallop, then replace the top. Dollop 1 teaspoon of purée on each potato crisp, then top with a filled scallop. Season with pepper and garnish with mint.

Makes 24

scallops on potato crisps with pea purée

baby caviar potatoes

30 baby new potatoes (choose
   very small potatoes of a
   similar size)
250 g (9 oz/1 cup) sour cream

2 tablespoons caviar
   (red or black, or both)

Preheat the oven to 200°C (400°F/Gas 6). Prick the potatoes with a fork and put them on a baking tray. Bake for 40 minutes, or until tender. Cool to room temperature.

Cut a large cross in the top of each potato and squeeze open. Top with a small dollop of sour cream and a little caviar.

Makes 30

chicken and tarragon cream vol au vents

1 small chicken breast fillet
250 ml (9 fl oz/1 cup) pure
   (single) cream
1 tablespoon finely chopped
   tarragon

1 spring onion (scallion), finely
   chopped
12 mini vol au vent pastry shells

Put the chicken fillet in a small saucepan of salted boiling water. Cover, turn off the heat and poach the chicken for about 20 minutes. Remove and cool before cutting the chicken into very small cubes. Preheat the oven to 170°C (325°F/Gas 3).

Put the cream in a small saucepan and bring to boiling point. Reduce the heat and simmer for 5–10 minutes, or until the cream is very thick. Stir in the chicken, tarragon and spring onion. While still warm, spoon the filling into the pastry shells, piling the filling up. Bake for 8 minutes. Serve hot.

Makes 12

When an occasion calls for something special but funds are low, mussels bring a little seafood luxury without breaking the bank.

herbed mussel tarts

2 kg (4 lb 8 oz) black mussels
90 g (3¼ oz) butter, softened
2 garlic cloves, crushed
2 tablespoons chopped chives
2 tablespoons chopped flat-leaf (Italian) parsley
24 slices white bread
60 g (2¼ oz) butter, extra, melted

Preheat the oven to 180°C (350°F/Gas 4). Scrub the mussels with a stiff brush and pull out the hairy beards. Discard any broken mussels, or open ones that don't close when tapped on a bench. Rinse well. Bring 500 ml (17 fl oz/2 cups) of water to the boil in a large saucepan, add half the mussels and cook, covered, for 3–5 minutes, or until just opened. Discard any unopened mussels. Repeat with the remaining mussels, then cover immediately with cold water and remove the flesh from the shells (if the mussels are very large, cut them in half). Pat dry with paper towels.

Beat the butter until smooth, stir in the garlic, chives and parsley and season with salt and pepper.

Flatten the bread slices with a rolling pin and, using an 8 cm (3¹/4 inch) cutter, cut a circle from each slice. Brush both sides of each circle with the melted butter, then press into 24 round-based patty tins. Bake for about 8 minutes, or until crisp and lightly golden.

Divide the mussels among the hot bread cases and carefully spread the herb butter over the top. Bake for 5 minutes, or until the mussels are heated through. Serve immediately.

Makes 24

chicken and tarragon cream
vol au vents

wrapped prawns with mango dip

24 snowpeas (mangetout)
24 medium cooked prawns
    (shrimp), peeled and
    deveined

mango dip
125 g (4^1/2 fl oz/^{1}/2 cup)
    mayonnaise
2 tablespoons mango chutney
1 teaspoon curry paste
1 tablespoon lime juice

Blanch the snowpeas in boiling water for 30 seconds, or until tender. Drain and cool. Wrap them around the cooked prawns, then secure each one with a toothpick.

To make the dip, mix together the mayonnaise, mango chutney, curry paste and lime juice. Serve with the prawns.

Makes 24

grilled figs in prosciutto

25 g (1 oz) unsalted butter
1 tablespoon orange juice
12 small fresh figs
12 sage leaves

6 slices of prosciutto, trimmed
and halved lengthways

Put the butter in a small heavy-based saucepan. Melt over low heat, then cook the butter for 8–10 minutes, or until the froth subsides and the milk solids appear as brown specks on the bottom of the saucepan. Strain the butter into a clean bowl by pouring it through a strainer lined with a clean tea towel or paper towel. Stir the orange juice into the strained butter.

Gently cut a cross in the crown of each fig, cutting two-thirds of the way through. Gently squeeze the base — the top will open like a flower. Sit a sage leaf in the opening of each fig, then wrap a piece of prosciutto around each one, with the ends tucked under the bottom of the fig. Arrange the figs, cut-side-up, on a baking tray and brush lightly with the butter mixture.

Move the grill tray to its lowest position, then heat the grill (broiler) to hot. Put the tray of figs on the grill tray and cook for 1–1^{1}/2 minutes, or until the prosciutto is slightly crispy. Serve warm or at room temperature.

Makes 12

Tiny, delicate whitebait make delectable, crunchy fritters that truly deserve an excellent, home-made tartare sauce.

whitebait fritters with tartare sauce

125 g (4¹/₂ oz/1 cup) plain
(all-purpose) flour
1 large egg, lightly beaten
250 ml (9 fl oz/1 cup) iced water
3 tablespoons chopped flat-leaf
(Italian) parsley
3 teaspoons grated lemon zest
400 g (14 oz) whitebait
oil, for deep-frying

tartare sauce
2 egg yolks
1 teaspoon Dijon mustard
250 ml (9 fl oz/1 cup) olive oil
1 tablespoon lemon juice
2 tablespoons capers, rinsed,
drained and chopped
2 tablespoons chopped gherkins
1 tablespoon chopped flat-leaf
(Italian) parsley
1 tablespoon chopped tarragon

Sift the flour and a pinch of salt and pepper into a large bowl, make a well in the centre and add the egg. Whisk gently and gradually add the water, stirring constantly to a smooth batter. Stir in the parsley and lemon zest. Cover and refrigerate for 1 hour.

To make the tartare sauce, put the egg yolks and mustard in a food processor and pulse for 10 seconds. With the motor running, slowly add the oil in a thin stream until the mixture is thick and creamy. Add the lemon juice and 2 teaspoons of boiling water and pulse for 10 seconds. Transfer to a bowl, stir in the capers, gherkin, parsley and tarragon and season generously. Cover and refrigerate until needed.

Pat the whitebait dry, then gently stir them into the batter. Fill a large heavy-based saucepan one-third full of oil and heat to 190°C (375°F), or until a cube of bread dropped in the oil browns in 10 seconds. Put small tablespoons of batter into the pan, gently tossing the fritters in the oil. Cook for 2–3 minutes, or until the fritters are golden brown. Drain on crumpled paper towels and keep warm. Repeat with the remaining mixture. Serve immediately with the tartare sauce.

Makes about 50

grilled figs in prosciutto

chilli and lemon olives

500 g (1 lb 2 oz/2¾ cups)
  cured black olives
2 teaspoons finely grated
  lemon zest

2 teaspoons chopped oregano
3 teaspoons dried chilli flakes
olive oil, to cover

Combine the olives, lemon zest, oregano and chilli flakes. Transfer to a 750 ml (26 fl oz/3 cup) sterilized jar, and add enough olive oil to cover. Seal, then chill in the refrigerator for at least 2 days. Return to room temperature before serving.

Fills a 750 ml (26 fl oz/3 cup) jar

lemon olives with vermouth

3 tablespoons dry vermouth
1 tablespoon lemon juice
2 teaspoons shredded
   lemon zest

2 tablespoons extra virgin
   olive oil
170 g (6 oz/1 cup) Spanish
   green or stuffed olives

Combine the vermouth, lemon juice, lemon zest and oil. Rinse the olives and pat them dry, then add to the marinade and toss well. Cover and refrigerate overnight. Serve at room temperature.

Fills a 250 g (9 oz/1 1/3 cup) jar

Wrapping the scallops in strips of fresh vegetables seals in all the juices, leaving them moist and juicy when cooked.

herbed scallop kebabs

24 scallops
2 zucchini (courgettes)
2 carrots
6 large spring onions (scallions), green part only, halved
    lengthways, then cut into 8 cm (3¼ inch) lengths
20 g (¾ oz) butter, melted
2 teaspoons lemon juice
1 tablespoon white wine
2 teaspoons mixed dried herbs

Soak 24 wooden skewers in cold water for 1 hour. Line a baking tray with foil. Using a sharp knife, carefully cut the scallops from their shells and remove the vein and white muscle. Wash the scallops and pat dry with paper towels.

Using a vegetable peeler, cut the zucchini and carrots lengthways into thin ribbons. Plunge the vegetable strips into a bowl of boiling water, leave for 1 minute, then drain. Plunge into a bowl of iced water and leave until cold. Drain and pat dry with paper towels.

Roll each scallop in a strip of spring onion, carrot and zucchini and secure with a wooden skewer.

Combine the butter, lemon juice and wine in a small bowl. Brush over the scallops, then sprinkle with the herbs. Cook under a hot grill (broiler) or in a chargrill pan (griddle) for 2 minutes on each side, or until the scallops are tender and cooked through. Serve hot.

Makes 24

chilli and lemon olives

lemon olives with vermouth

pumpkin and hazelnut pesto bites

750 g (1 lb 10 oz) butternut
    pumpkin (squash), cut
    into 2.5 cm (1 inch) cubes
1^1/$_2$ tablespoons olive oil

hazelnut pesto
35 g (1^1/$_4$ oz/^{1}/$_4$ cup) toasted
    hazelnuts
35 g (1^1/$_4$ oz/1 cup) rocket
    (arugula)
1 tablespoon grated Parmesan
    cheese
3^1/$_2$ tablespoons olive oil

Preheat the oven to 200°C (400°F/Gas 6) and line a baking tray with baking paper. Toss the pumpkin cubes with the oil and some salt and pepper until evenly coated. Spread out on the baking tray and bake for 35 minutes, or until cooked.

To make the hazelnut pesto, process the hazelnuts, rocket, Parmesan and oil until they form a paste. Season to taste with salt and black pepper.

Spoon a small amount of the hazelnut pesto onto each piece of pumpkin and sprinkle with black pepper if desired. Serve warm or cold.

Makes about 20

feta, rocket and mushroom bruschetta

1 loaf Italian (ciabatta) bread
1 large garlic clove, peeled
extra virgin olive oil, to drizzle

topping
1 tablespoon olive oil
60 g (2 1/4 oz) butter
300 g (10 1/2 oz) Swiss brown
    mushrooms, quartered

2 garlic cloves, crushed
2 tablespoons roughly torn basil
150 g (5 1/2 oz) soft marinated
    feta cheese
50 g (1 3/4 oz/1 1/4 cups) baby
    rocket (arugula) leaves

Preheat the oven to 200°C (400°F/Gas 6). Slice the bread on the diagonal into 12 x 1 cm (1/2 inch) thick slices. Lay the bread slices out in a single layer on a baking tray and bake for 10–12 minutes, or until lightly golden. Remove from the oven. Cut the garlic clove in half and rub over one side of each slice of toast, then lightly drizzle with oil. Cut them in half.

To make the topping, heat the oil and butter in a frying pan over high heat. Cook the mushrooms for 3–4 minutes, then add the garlic and cook for 1 minute. Remove the pan from the heat, stir in the basil and season to taste. Spread the feta on the bruschetta, and add a few rocket leaves. Top with some fried mushrooms, and serve immediately.

Makes 24

It's only polite to thank your guests for coming, so why not
reward them the Thai way with these delicious money bags.

money bags

1 tablespoon peanut oil
4 red Asian shallots, finely chopped
2 garlic cloves, crushed
1 tablespoon grated fresh ginger
150 g (5¹/2 oz) minced (ground) chicken
150 g (5¹/2 oz) minced (ground) pork
2 teaspoons light soy sauce
40 g (1¹/2 oz/¹/4 cup) toasted peanuts, chopped
2 teaspoons grated palm sugar
2 teaspoons lime juice
3 teaspoons fish sauce
3 tablespoons finely chopped coriander (cilantro) leaves
30 won ton wrappers
oil, for deep-frying
garlic chives, for tying

Heat the oil in a frying pan over medium heat. Add the shallots, garlic and ginger and cook for 1–2 minutes, or until the shallots are soft. Add the chicken and pork and cook for 4 minutes, or until cooked, breaking up the lumps with a wooden spoon.

Stir in the soy sauce, chopped peanuts, palm sugar, lime juice, fish sauce and coriander. Cook, stirring, for 1–2 minutes, or until combined and dry. Leave to cool.

Put 2 teaspoons of the filling in the centre of each won ton wrapper, then lightly brush the edges with water. Lift the sides up tightly and pinch around the filling to form a bag. Trim.

Fill a deep heavy-based saucepan one-third full of oil and heat to 190°C (375°F), or until a cube of bread dropped in the oil browns in 10 seconds. Cook in batches for 30–60 seconds, or until golden and crisp. Drain on paper towels. Tie with the garlic chives and serve.

Makes 30

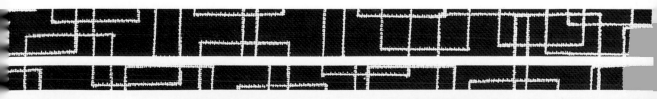

pumpkin and hazelnut pesto bites

parmesan wafers

125 g (4¹/2 oz/1¹/4 cups) grated good-quality Parmesan cheese	1 tablespoon flour 2 tablespoons thyme

Preheat the oven to 220°C (425°F/Gas 7). Line two baking trays with baking paper and, using a 7 cm (2³/4 inch) cutter as a guide, draw circles on the paper. Turn the paper upside down on the trays. Toss the cheese and flour together in a bowl, then sprinkle 2 teaspoons of the mixture over three or four circles on the paper, spreading the mixture to the edge of each round. Scatter a few thyme leaves over each round.

Bake in batches for 3 minutes, or until melted but not firm. Using a spatula, turn the rounds over and cook for 1 minute more, or until they are firm and light golden. Remove each round from the tray and drape over a rolling pin or bottle until cool. Repeat to make 30 wafers.

Makes 30

olive basil cheese spread

250 g (9 oz/1 cup) cream cheese, softened
200 g (7 oz/1⅓ cups) feta cheese, crumbled

1 large handful basil leaves
3 tablespoons olive oil
15 Kalamata olives, pitted and roughly chopped

Combine the cream cheese, feta, basil, 1 tablespoon of the olive oil and ¼ teaspoon of cracked black pepper in a bowl and mix until smooth.

Fold in the olives and spoon into a serving bowl. Smooth the top with the back of the spoon. Pour the remaining oil over the top and garnish with a little more cracked pepper. Delicious served with warm bread.

Serves 6–8

hot corn cakes with avocado and prawns

avocado sauce
1 ripe avocado, roughly chopped
2 tablespoons lime juice
1 tinned chipotle pepper, in sauce
1 handful coriander (cilantro) leaves
1 garlic clove, chopped
1 teaspoon ground cumin
2 tablespoons sour cream

60 g (2^1/$_4$ oz/^{1}/$_2$ cup) plain (all-purpose) flour
50 g (1^3/$_4$ oz/^{1}/$_3$ cup) polenta
^{1}/$_2$ teaspoon baking powder
^{1}/$_4$ teaspoon bicarbonate of soda
1 teaspoon salt
^{1}/$_2$ teaspoon sugar
250 ml (9 fl oz/1 cup) buttermilk
20 g (^{3}/$_4$ oz) butter, melted
1 egg
110 g (3^3/$_4$ oz/^{3}/$_4$ cup) frozen corn kernels, thawed, chopped
1^1/$_2$ tinned chipotle peppers, chopped, and 2 teaspoons of sauce
32 cooked prawns (shrimp), peeled and deveined
^{1}/$_2$ lime, sliced very thinly, cut into 32 small wedges, to garnish

To make the avocado sauce, put the ingredients and $^{1}/_{2}$ teaspoon of salt in a food processor and purée until very smooth. Season.

Combine the dry ingredients in a large bowl and make a well in the centre. Whisk the buttermilk, butter and egg together in a jug, gradually add to the dry ingredients and whisk until thoroughly incorporated. Roughly chop the corn and chipotle peppers in a food processor, then stir into the batter. (The batter should have the consistency of pancake batter — add a tablespoon of water to thin if necessary.)

Heat a lightly oiled frying pan over medium heat. Spoon tablespoons of the batter into the pan in batches, forming 5 cm (2 inch) cakes. Cook for 1 minute on each side, or until golden brown. Remove from the pan and keep warm while cooking the rest of the corn cakes.

Dollop a heaped teaspoon of avocado sauce on the warm corn cakes. Put one prawn on top and garnish with a tiny wedge of lime.

Makes 32

hot corn cakes with
avocado and prawns

beef rolls

500 g (1 lb 2 oz) beef fillet,
    8 cm (3¹/₄ inches) in diameter
3 tablespoons olive oil
1¹/₂ tablespoons horseradish
    cream
1¹/₂ tablespoons wholegrain
    mustard
1 zucchini (courgette), cut into
    thin strips

1 small carrot, cut into thin
    strips
1 small red capsicum (pepper),
    cut into thin strips
60 g (2¹/₄ oz) snowpeas
    (mangetout), cut into
    thin strips

Preheat the oven to 200°C (400°F/Gas 6). Trim the beef of excess fat and sinew and brush with a little of the oil. Heat a heavy-based frying pan over high heat and quickly brown each side of the beef fillet. Transfer to a baking dish and bake for 20 minutes. Remove and set aside to cool.

Slice the cooled beef very thinly. Combine the horseradish cream and the mustard, then spread a little over each slice of beef.

Heat the remaining oil in a saucepan over high heat and quickly cook the zucchini, carrot, capsicum and snowpeas. Cool. Put a small bunch of the vegetable strips on the end of each beef slice and roll up. Serve.

Makes about 20

devils and angels on horseback

4–6 streaky bacon rashers,
    cut into thin strips
12 pitted prunes
12 oysters, fresh or bottled

2 tablespoons Worcestershire
    sauce
Tabasco sauce, to taste

Soak 24 toothpicks in cold water for 1 hour to prevent them burning.

To make the devils, wrap a piece of bacon around each prune and secure with a skewer.

To make the angels, remove the oysters from their shells, or drain from the bottling liquid. Sprinkle lightly with Worcestershire sauce and some black pepper. Wrap each oyster in bacon, securing with a toothpick.

Preheat a lightly greased grill (broiler) or barbecue flatplate. Cook the savouries, turning occasionally, until the bacon is crisp. Serve sprinkled with a dash of Tabasco sauce.

Makes 24

mini crab cakes with coriander paste

20 g (3/4 oz) butter
4 spring onions (scallions), thinly sliced
1 egg
2 tablespoons sour cream
350 g (12 oz) fresh white crab meat, excess liquid squeezed out
1 small yellow capsicum (pepper), finely diced
2 teaspoons chopped thyme
120 g (4 oz/1 1/2 cups) fresh white breadcrumbs
olive oil, for pan-frying

coriander paste
1 garlic clove
1 green chilli, seeded
1/2 teaspoon ground cumin
1/4 teaspoon sugar
1 large handful coriander (cilantro) leaves
1 handful mint leaves
1 tablespoon lemon juice
25 ml (1 fl oz) coconut cream
1/2 avocado

Line a tray with baking paper. Melt the butter in a frying pan over low heat. When it begins to foam, add the spring onion and cook for about 1–2 minutes, or until softened. Remove from the heat and cool.

Put the egg and sour cream in a bowl and mix until just smooth. Add the cooled spring onion, crab meat, capsicum, thyme and breadcrumbs, season and mix together. Shape the mixture into flat rounds, using 1 level tablespoon of the mixture for each round. Put the crab cakes on the lined tray and refrigerate for 30 minutes.

To make the coriander paste, put the garlic, chilli, cumin, sugar, herbs, lemon juice and 1/4 teaspoon of salt in a food processor and blend to a fine paste. Add the coconut cream and continue to blend until smooth. Add the avocado and, using the pulse action, process until just smooth. Transfer to a small bowl, cover with plastic wrap and refrigerate.

Heat enough olive oil in a non-stick frying pan to just coat the bottom. Cook the crab cakes in batches for 2–3 minutes on each side, or until golden. Drain and serve warm with 1/2 teaspoon of coriander paste on each cake.

Makes 24

mini crab cakes with coriander paste

salt and pepper squid

1 kg (2 lb 4 oz) small squid
  tubes
250 ml (9 fl oz/1 cup) lemon
  juice
250 g (9 oz/2 cups) cornflour
  (cornstarch)
2 tablespoons salt

1¹/₂ tablespoons ground white
  pepper
2 teaspoons caster (superfine)
  sugar
oil, for deep-frying
4 egg whites, lightly beaten

Wash and pat dry the squid tubes and cut into thin rings. Put the rings in a flat non-metallic dish and pour the lemon juice over the top. Cover and refrigerate for 15 minutes. Drain and pat dry.

Combine the cornflour, salt, pepper and sugar in a bowl. Fill a deep heavy-based saucepan one-third full of oil and heat to 180°C (350°F), or until a cube of bread dropped in the oil browns in 15 seconds. Dip the squid into the egg white and dust with the salt and pepper mixture, shaking off any excess. Add the squid to the oil in batches and deep-fry for 1–2 minutes, or until golden. Serve immediately.

Serves 8–10

thai chicken cakes

4 eggs, lightly beaten
2 tablespoons finely chopped
    coriander (cilantro) leaves
1 tablespoon fish sauce
2 tablespoons oil
500 g (1 lb 2 oz) minced
    (ground) chicken
3 stems lemon grass, white
    part only, finely chopped
2 garlic cloves, crushed
4 spring onions (scallions),
    chopped

3 tablespoons lime juice
1 large handful coriander
    (cilantro) leaves and stems,
    extra, chopped
2 tablespoons sweet chilli sauce
1 tablespoon fish sauce
1 egg, extra, lightly beaten
125 ml (4 fl oz/1/2 cup) coconut
    milk
6 red chillies, seeded and finely
    sliced

Preheat the oven to 200°C (400°F/Gas 6). Lightly grease three 12-hole shallow patty tins. In a bowl combine the eggs, coriander and fish sauce. Heat the oil in a large frying pan over medium heat, add the egg mixture and cook for 2 minutes each side, or until golden. Roll up and shred finely.

Process the chicken, lemon grass, garlic, spring onion, lime juice, extra coriander, sauces, extra egg and coconut milk in a food processor until fine but not smooth. Spoon into the patty tins and top with the shredded omelette. Bake for 15 minutes, or until cooked. Rotate the trays once to ensure the cakes cook through evenly. Serve hot, garnished with chilli.

Makes 36

Cool as a cucumber — this is a great way to soften the sting of chilli and make a crispy serving cup for tender strips of beef.

cucumber cups with thai beef salad

4 Lebanese (short) cucumbers
oil, for pan-frying
250 g (9 oz) beef fillet steak
1/2 red onion, finely chopped
20 mint leaves, finely chopped
1 tablespoon finely chopped coriander (cilantro) leaves
11/2 tablespoons fish sauce
11/2 tablespoons lime juice
1 small red chilli, seeded and finely chopped
1 teaspoon grated palm sugar or soft brown sugar
24 small coriander (cilantro) leaves, extra

Trim each end of the cucumbers but do not peel them. Cut each cucumber into 2 cm (3/4 inch) thick slices; you should get 24 pieces. Scoop out the centre of each slice with a melon baller, leaving a shell of flesh.

Heat a large frying pan over high heat and brush lightly with oil. Season the beef with salt and pepper, then add to the pan and cook for about 1^1/$_2$–2 minutes on each side, depending on the thickness (the beef needs to be rare). Rest for 5 minutes. Thinly slice the beef across the grain, then cut each piece into 5 mm (^{1}/$_4$ inch) wide strips and transfer to a bowl.

Add the onion, mint and coriander to the bowl and mix well.

Combine the fish sauce, lime juice, chilli and sugar in a small bowl and stir until the sugar has dissolved. Pour over the beef mixture and mix until well combined. Fill each cucumber cup with a little Thai beef salad and garnish each one with a whole coriander leaf.

Makes 24

salt and pepper squid

lounge Late night grooves and low-key lounging with a group of your closest friends require a special kind of sustenance to keep the party going. Throw away the take-out menus and indulge

your guests with a grown-up midnight feast. Forget the rule book and let the late hour create a magic all of its own. At this time of night, you can get away with anything.

Late-night lounging is distinct from the cocktail hour in several fundamental ways, aside from the lateness of the hour. While cocktails are about lots of people mingling, lounging is about a small group of friends gathering for some laid-back late-night revelling. Whether you're planning to cater for the post-pub or pre-club crowd, the food should be substantial and the drinks simple and plentiful. Late-night grooves are the inspiration for this type of event and you should think of it as being more like a meal than any of the others. The dishes you serve your guests should work together as well as being delicious on their own and it's a good idea to plan around leaving yourself free to sit and relax with your friends as much as possible. The aim of lounging is not to impress but to create an atmosphere that is sophisticated and relaxed, stimulating and chilled, with food that stimulates the senses while the setting and the ambient music create a feeling of relaxation. There is a definite retro chic aesthetic associated with late-night lounging: think of the fifties — the era of crooners, lounge clubs and hard liquor — as a source of inspiration when it comes to decorating and serving the food. Pull out the hostess trolley, dig out some angular, graphic servingware and give it a modern twist by matching it with cutting-edge food and music. Conjure up that lounging mood and kick back into a spot of cruisy, late-night lounging.

thai fish cakes

500 g (1 lb 2 oz) firm white fish fillets, skin removed
1¹/2 tablespoons red curry paste
55 g (2 oz/¹/4 cup) sugar
3 tablespoons fish sauce
1 egg
100 g (3¹/2 oz) snake beans, thinly sliced
10 makrut (kaffir lime) leaves, finely chopped
oil, for deep-frying
sweet chilli sauce, to serve

Put the fish in a food processor and process until smooth. Add the curry paste, sugar, fish sauce and egg. Process for another 10 seconds, or until combined. Stir in the beans and lime leaves. Shape the mixture into walnut-sized balls, then flatten them into patties.

Fill a wok one-third full of oil and heat to 180°C (350°F), or until a cube of bread dropped in the oil browns in 15 seconds. Cook in batches for 3–5 minutes, turning occasionally. Drain on crumpled paper towels. Serve hot with sweet chilli sauce.

Makes 24

lime prawns

6 tinned sugar canes
48 raw king prawns (shrimp),
   peeled and deveined
125 ml (4 fl oz/½ cup) lime juice
lime wedges, to serve

Cut the sugar canes into 5 mm (¼ inch) thick strips 10 cm (4 inches) long. Thread two prawns onto each sugar cane skewer (you may need to make small cuts in the prawns to make this easier).

Brush the prawns lightly with lime juice and cook in a hot lightly oiled chargrill pan (griddle) for 2–3 minutes each side, or until the prawns are cooked through. Serve with lime wedges.

Makes 24

Fresh basil butter brings out the delicate flavour of fresh mussels so easily drowned by heavier sauces.

basil mussels

1 kg (2 lb 4 oz) black mussels
10 g (1/4 oz) butter
2 red Asian shallots, chopped
125 ml (4 fl oz/1/2 cup) dry white wine

basil butter
50 g (1 3/4 oz) butter
1 handful basil
1 garlic clove, chopped
2 tablespoons dry breadcrumbs

Scrub the mussels with a stiff brush and pull out the hairy beards. Discard any broken mussels or open ones that don't close when tapped on the bench. Rinse well.

Melt the butter in a large saucepan over medium heat. Add the shallots and cook for 2 minutes, or until soft. Add the wine and mussels, increase the heat and cook for 4–5 minutes, stirring occasionally, until the mussels have opened. Remove the open mussels and discard any unopened ones.

To make the basil butter, put all the ingredients in a food processor or blender and process until smooth. Season with ground black pepper.

Separate the mussel shells, leaving the meat on one half. Discard the empty shells. Put a teaspoon of basil butter on each mussel. Arrange on a foil-lined grill (broiler) tray and cook under a hot grill for 1 minute, or until the butter has melted. Season with salt and black pepper, to taste.

Serves 6

lime prawns

oysters with pine nuts and bacon

24 fresh oysters on the half shell
2 rindless rashers of bacon
30 g (1 oz) butter
1 small onion, finely chopped
100 g (3 1/2 oz/1 small bunch)
   rocket (arugula), leaves torn

2 teaspoons Worcestershire
   sauce
2 tablespoons toasted pine nuts,
   roughly chopped

Remove the oysters from their shells, then cover and refrigerate until needed. Wash the shells in hot water and pat dry.

Cook the bacon under a preheated grill (broiler) until crisp. Cool, then break into small shards.

Melt the butter in a frying pan, add the onion and cook, stirring, until soft. Add the rocket and cook until just wilted. Stir in the Worcestershire sauce.

Divide the rocket mixture among the oyster shells, return the oysters to the shells and top with the bacon shards. Scatter the pine nuts over the top and serve warm or cold.

Makes 24

grilled prawns with tequila mayonnaise

4 tablespoons olive oil
2 tablespoons lime juice
24 raw king prawns (shrimp),
   peeled and deveined,
   tails intact
1 tablespoon tequila

160 g (5^3/$_4$ oz/^{2}/$_3$ cup)
   whole-egg mayonnaise

Combine the olive oil and lime juice in a non-metallic bowl and season well. Add the prawns, cover and refrigerate for 1 hour.

Mix the tequila into the mayonnaise, then transfer to a serving dish.

Heat a barbecue hot plate or chargrill pan (griddle) to hot, add the prawns and cook for 1–2 minutes on each side, or until pink and cooked through. Serve with the tequila mayonnaise for dipping.

Makes 24

risotto cakes with preserved lemon mayonnaise

1 litre (35 fl oz/4 cups) chicken stock
1 tablespoon olive oil
1 garlic clove, finely chopped
1 small onion, finely chopped
220 g (8 oz/1 cup) arborio rice
125 ml (4 fl oz/^{1}/2 cup) dry white wine
4 marinated artichokes, drained and finely chopped
25 g (1 oz/^{1}/4 cup) coarsely grated Parmesan cheese
1 teaspoon grated lemon zest
60 g (2^1/4 oz/^{1}/2 cup) plain (all-purpose) flour
2 eggs, beaten
100 g (3^1/2 oz/1 cup) dry breadcrumbs
3 slices pancetta
90 g (3^1/4 oz/^{1}/3 cup) whole-egg mayonnaise
2 teaspoons finely chopped preserved lemon peel
oil, for pan-frying
15 pitted Kalamata olives, halved
flat-leaf (Italian) parsley, to garnish

Pour the stock into a saucepan and keep at a low simmer. Heat the oil in a saucepan over low heat and cook the garlic and onion for 4–5 minutes, or until softened. Stir in the rice for 1 minute, or until well coated in the oil. Add the wine and stir over medium heat until it has all been absorbed. Add 125 ml (4 fl oz/1/2 cup) of stock, and stir constantly until it is nearly absorbed. Continue adding the stock, 125 ml (4 fl oz/1/2 cup) at a time, stirring constantly until it is completely absorbed before the next addition. The risotto will be ready after 20 minutes when the rice is tender and the mixture appears creamy. Stir in the artichoke, Parmesan and lemon zest. Spread the risotto out on a tray and leave to cool for 2 hours.

Put the flour in one bowl, the egg in another and the breadcrumbs in a third. Using wet hands, roll the risotto into 30 discs 3 cm (1 1/4 inch) across and 1.5 cm (5/8 inch) high. Coat them with flour, dip them in egg, then coat them in the breadcrumbs. Refrigerate for at least 30 minutes.

Cook the pancetta in a non-stick frying pan until crisp, then tear each slice into 10 pieces. Mix together the mayonnaise and preserved lemon.

Heat the oil in a frying pan, add the risotto cakes in batches and cook for 2–3 minutes on each side, or until golden and crisp. Drain on paper towels. Top each risotto cake with 1/2 teaspoon of the lemon mayonnaise, a piece of pancetta, half an olive and a torn parsley leaf. Serve warm or hot.

Makes 30

Cocktail

oysters with pine nuts and bacon

lemon grass prawns

6 stems lemon grass, halved,
    then cut in half lengthways
1 kg (2 lb 4 oz) prawns (shrimp),
    peeled and deveined
3 spring onions (scallions),
    roughly chopped
4 tablespoons coriander
    (cilantro) leaves

2 tablespoons mint leaves
2 tablespoons fish sauce
1 1/2 tablespoons lime juice
1–2 tablespoons sweet chilli
    sauce, plus extra for serving
peanut oil, for brushing

Soak the lemon grass in water for 30 minutes, then pat dry. Put the prawns, spring onion, coriander, mint, fish sauce, lime juice and sweet chilli sauce in a food processor and process until smooth. Using wet hands, mould 1 tablespoon of the mixture around the end of each lemon grass stem. Refrigerate for 30 minutes.

Brush a barbecue hotplate or chargrill pan (griddle) with the peanut oil. Cook the skewers, turning occasionally, for 5 minutes, or until cooked. Serve with sweet chilli sauce.

Makes 24

sesame beef skewers

125 ml (4 fl oz/1/2 cup) soy sauce
4 tablespoons Chinese rice wine
2 garlic cloves, crushed
1 teaspoon finely grated fresh
  ginger
1 teaspoon sesame oil

225 g (8 oz) scotch fillet, cut
  into 2 cm (3/4 inch) cubes
8 spring onions (scallions)
2 tablespoons toasted sesame
  seeds

Combine the soy sauce, rice wine, garlic, ginger and sesame oil, and pour over the beef. Marinate for 20 minutes. Drain, reserving the marinade.

Cut six of the spring onions into 24 pieces, 3 cm (1 1/4 inch) in length. Thread one piece of spring onion and two beef cubes onto 24 metal skewers. Cook on a hot barbecue hotplate or chargrill pan (griddle) for about 5 minutes, or until cooked. Remove, sprinkle with sesame seeds and keep warm.

Put the reserved marinade in a saucepan. Bring to the boil for 1 minute, then add two thinly sliced spring onions. Serve with the skewers.

Makes 24

pork and peanut dip

paste
2 small dried red chillies
2 teaspoons chopped coriander (cilantro) root
3 teaspoons ground white pepper
6 garlic cloves, chopped
4 red Asian shallots, chopped

1 tablespoon peanut oil, plus extra for deep-frying
300 g (10$^{1}/_{2}$ oz) minced (ground) pork
2 makrut (kaffir lime) leaves
250 ml (9 fl oz/1 cup) coconut cream
50 g (1$^{3}/_{4}$ oz/$^{1}/_{3}$ cup) peanuts, toasted and chopped
1$^{1}/_{2}$ tablespoons lime juice
3 tablespoons fish sauce
2 tablespoons grated palm sugar
1 tablespoon finely shredded Thai basil leaves
150 g (5$^{1}/_{2}$ oz) cassava crackers

To make the paste, put the chillies in a bowl of boiling water and soak for about 15 minutes. Remove the seeds and chop the flesh. Put all the paste ingredients in a food processor and blend until smooth (add a little water if necessary).

Heat the peanut oil in a saucepan over medium heat. Add the paste and cook, stirring frequently, for 15 minutes, or until the paste darkens.

Add the pork and stir for 5 minutes, or until it changes colour. Stir in the lime leaves and coconut cream, scraping the base of the pan. Cook for 40 minutes, stirring frequently, until almost all the liquid has evaporated. Add the peanuts, lime juice, fish sauce and palm sugar and cook for about 10 minutes, or until the oil begins to separate. Remove from the heat, remove the lime leaves and stir in the basil.

329

Fill a deep heavy-based saucepan one-third full of oil and heat to 180°C (350°F), or until a cube of bread dropped in the oil browns in 15 seconds. Break the cassava crackers in half and deep-fry in small batches until pale and golden — they will puff up quickly, so remove immediately. Drain on paper towels. Serve with the pork and peanut dip.

Serves 6–8

lemon grass prawn

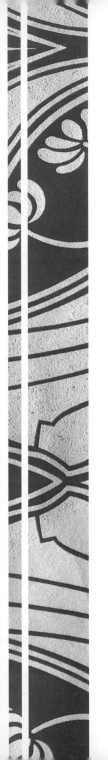

bocconcini, tomato and sun-dried capsicum salsa

175 g (6 oz) fresh bocconcini chese, cut into 1 cm (1/2 inch) dice

2 large tomatoes, cut into 1 cm (1/2 inch) dice

50 g (13/4 oz/1/3 cup) drained sun-dried capsicums (peppers) in oil, chopped

1 spring onion (scallion), finely sliced

1 tablespoon extra virgin olive oil

2 teaspoons red wine vinegar

1 tablespoon shredded basil

1 tablespoon chopped flat-leaf (Italian) parsley

Mix together the bocconcini, tomato, sun-dried capsicum and spring onion in a large bowl.

Whisk together the oil and red wine vinegar until thoroughly blended. Stir in the basil and parsley.

Toss the dressing through the bocconcini and tomato mixture and season with salt and black pepper. Serve at room temperature with small toasts.

Serves 6

green mexican salsa

300 g (10¹/₂ oz) tin tomatillos,
   drained
1 small onion, chopped
1 jalapeño chilli, finely chopped
3 garlic cloves, crushed

2 tablespoons chopped
   coriander (cilantro) leaves
1–2 teaspoons lime juice

Put the tomatillos in a food processor with the onion, chilli, garlic and 1 tablespoon of the coriander. Process until smooth, then blend in the lime juice, to taste. Add the rest of the coriander and process just long enough to mix it through the dip. Delicious served with corn chips.

Serves 6–8

333

Cute as a button and undeniably ladylike, we defy you to show any restraint when faced with a platter of these burgers.

mini hamburgers

8 burger buns, split in half
(or Turkish bread)
400 g (14 oz) minced (ground)
beef
25 g (1 oz/¼ cup) dry
breadcrumbs
3 French shallots, very finely
chopped
1 tablespoon Dijon mustard
1 tablespoon Worcestershire
sauce
4 tablespoons tomato sauce

olive oil, for pan-frying
100 g (3½ oz) thinly sliced
Cheddar cheese, cut into
24 squares, each 3 cm
(1¼ inches)
24 baby rocket (arugula) leaves,
stems removed and torn into
2.5 cm (1 inch) pieces
½ small red onion, thinly sliced
12 cornichons (baby gherkins),
cut in half

Stamp out rounds from the burger buns using a 4 cm (1½ inch) cutter; you should get 24 from the tops and 24 from the bases. If your buns are quite thick, trim them with a serrated knife after you have cut them.

Combine the beef, breadcrumbs, shallots, mustard, Worcestershire sauce, 1 tablespoon of the tomato sauce and some salt and cracked black pepper in a bowl. Divide the mixture into 24 walnut-sized pieces. With wet hands, shape the pieces into balls, then flatten into patties.

Heat a large heavy-based frying pan with enough oil to just cover the bottom of the pan. Cook the patties over medium heat for 1–2 minutes on each side, or until browned and cooked to your liking.

Top each bun base with a cheese square and grill for 1 minute, or until the cheese is just starting to melt. Lightly grill the bun tops.

Put the patties on the bun bases and top with the remaining tomato sauce, the rocket and onion. Gently press on the bun tops and secure with a cocktail stick stuck through a cornichon half. Serve warm.

Makes 24

mini hamburgers

crispy vermicelli cakes with sesame vegetables

oil, for pan-frying
400 g (14 oz) dried rice
    vermicelli, soaked in boiling
    water for 3 minutes, then
    drained until very dry
2 teaspoons sesame oil
2 carrots, cut into julienne strips

1 red capsicum (pepper),
    cut into julienne strips
2 zucchini (courgettes),
    cut into julienne strips
4 spring onions (scallions),
    cut into julienne strips
1/2–1 tablespoon oyster sauce

Heat the oil in a large heavy-based frying pan over medium heat. Shape tablespoons of the noodles into flat discs, add to the pan in batches and cook for 3 minutes, or until crisp and golden. Drain on paper towels.

Heat the sesame oil in a wok and stir-fry the vegetables for 3 minutes, or until slightly softened. Stir in the oyster sauce and cook for 2 minutes. Spoon the vegetables over the noodle cakes and serve.

Makes about 12

salmon carpaccio with pear, caperberry and cress

200 g (7 oz) salmon fillet
1 pear, cut into julienne strips
4 caperberries, cut into quarters

small handful mustard cress
extra virgin olive oil, for drizzling
2 lemons

Slice the salmon very thinly and divide the slices among 16 small Chinese soup spoons. Top each spoon with a few strips of pear, a caperberry quarter and a few sprigs of mustard cress. Drizzle with some extra virgin olive oil, a squeeze of lemon juice and black pepper.

Makes 16

These little pockets are full of colour and bursting with heat, thanks to the combination of jalapeño chillies, olives and herbs.

mini spicy pork quesadillas

2^3/$_4$ tablespoons olive oil
^{1}/$_2$ teaspoon ground oregano
1 teaspoon ground cumin
^{1}/$_2$ teaspoon garlic salt
^{1}/$_2$ teaspoon cayenne pepper
350 g (12 oz) minced (ground) pork
2–3 jalapeño chillies in brine, chopped
30 g (1 oz/^{1}/$_4$ cup) pitted black olives, sliced
55 g (2 oz/^{1}/$_3$ cup) green olives stuffed with
    red pimentos, sliced
2 tablespoons chopped coriander (cilantro) leaves
12 x 16 cm (6^1/$_4$ inch) flour tortillas, cut in half
60 g (2^1/$_4$ oz/^{1}/$_2$ cup) grated mild Cheddar cheese
75 g (2^1/$_2$ oz/^{1}/$_2$ cup) grated mozzarella cheese
coriander (cilantro) sprigs, to garnish

Heat 1^1/$_2$ tablespoons of the oil in a large frying pan. When hot, add the oregano, cumin, garlic salt and cayenne pepper and cook for 30 seconds. Add the pork and cook over high heat for 10 minutes, before adding the chilli and all the olives. Cook for another 5 minutes, then stir in the chopped coriander. Remove from the heat and allow to cool.

Put 1 tablespoon of filling on one half of each tortilla half. Mix the cheeses together, then put 1 tablespoon of the cheese on top of the spicy pork mixture. Turn the flap of tortilla over the filling and press down firmly.

Heat 2 teaspoons of the remaining oil in a non-stick frying pan over high heat, add the quesadillas in batches and cook for 3–4 minutes on each side, or until golden. Add a teaspoon of oil to the pan after each batch. Garnish with coriander sprigs and serve hot.

Makes 24

salmon carpaccio with pear,
caperberry and cress

basic pizza dough

7 g sachet dried yeast
1/2 teaspoon caster (superfine) sugar

250 g (9 oz/2 cups) plain (all-purpose) flour
1 tablespoon olive oil

Mix the yeast, sugar and 185 ml (6 fl oz/3/4 cup) of warm water in a small bowl, then cover and set aside for 10 minutes, or until frothy. If it hasn't foamed after 10 minutes, the yeast is dead so you will have to start again.

Sift the flour and 1/2 teaspoon of salt into a large bowl and make a well in the centre. Pour in the yeast mixture and add the oil. Mix with a flat-bladed knife, using a cutting action, until a dough forms. Turn out onto a lightly floured work surface and knead for 10 minutes, or until smooth. Transfer to a large lightly oiled bowl, cover with plastic wrap and leave for 45 minutes, or until it has doubled in size.

Preheat the oven to 230°C (450°F/Gas 8). Punch down the dough, then knead for 8 minutes, or until elastic. Divide the dough into 24 portions and roll each portion into a ball. Use a rolling pin to roll each ball into a circle 3–4 mm (1/8 inch) thick and 4.5 cm (13/4 inches) in diameter. Prick the surfaces with a fork and brush with oil. Keep any unrolled balls covered so that they do not dry out. Put the pizza bases on a lightly greased baking tray, top with your filling and bake for 8–10 minutes.

Makes 24 round mini pizza bases

turkish pizza

3 teaspoons olive oil, plus
    extra for brushing
200 g (7 oz) minced (ground)
    lamb
1 small onion, finely chopped
2 tablespoons pine nuts
1 small tomato, peeled, seeded
    and chopped
1/4 teaspoon ground cinnamon

pinch of allspice
1 1/2 teaspoons chopped
    coriander (cilantro) leaves
1 1/2 teaspoons lemon juice
1 quantity pizza dough
    (see facing page)
3 tablespoons plain yoghurt

Preheat the oven to 230°C (450°F/Gas 8). Heat the oil in a frying pan over medium heat and cook the lamb for 3 minutes, or until it browns. Add the onion and cook over low heat for 6–8 minutes, or until soft. Add the pine nuts, tomato, spices, 1/4 teaspoon of black pepper and some salt. Cook for 8 minutes, or until dry. Stir in the coriander and lemon juice.

Divide the pizza dough into 18 portions and roll into oval shapes. Spoon some of the filling onto the centre of each pizza base. Draw up and pinch together the two short sides to form a boat shape, then brush with oil. Put the pizzas on a lightly greased baking tray and bake for 8–10 minutes. Spoon 1/2 teaspoon yoghurt on each pizza and serve hot.

Makes 18

mini polenta muffins with cajun fish

muffins
90 g (3^1/$_4$ oz/^{3}/$_4$ cup) self-raising flour
2 tablespoons cornflour (cornstarch)
^{1}/$_2$ teaspoon baking powder
75 g (2^1/$_2$ oz/^{1}/$_2$ cup) fine polenta
2 tablespoons sugar
170 ml (5^1/$_2$ fl oz/^{2}/$_3$ cup) milk
1 egg
30 g (1 oz) butter, melted
20 g (^{3}/$_4$ oz) butter, extra

1 teaspoon onion powder
1 teaspoon dried thyme
^{3}/$_4$ teaspoon sea salt flakes
^{1}/$_2$ teaspoon garlic powder
^{1}/$_4$ teaspoon cayenne pepper
^{1}/$_4$ teaspoon dried oregano

400 g (14 oz) firm white fish fillets, skinned
30 g (1 oz) butter
125 g (4^1/$_2$ oz/^{1}/$_2$ cup) sour cream
coriander (cilantro) leaves, to garnish

Preheat the oven to 180°C (350°F/Gas 4). Grease 24 non-stick mini muffin holes. To make the muffins, sift the flour, cornflour and baking powder into a bowl. Stir in the polenta and sugar. Make a well in the centre. Pour in the combined milk and egg, then the melted butter. Fold gently with a metal spoon until just combined and a little lumpy. Fill each muffin hole about three-quarters full. Bake for 15–20 minutes, or until golden. Just before removing from the oven, melt the extra butter and brush generously over the muffins. Remove from the tin and cool on a wire rack.

Combine the spices and herbs and $1/4$ teaspoon of cracked black pepper. Cut the fish into 1.5 cm ($5/8$ inch) slices and coat well in the spice mixture.

Melt the butter in a stainless steel frying pan (not non-stick) over medium heat and add the fish when the butter is foaming. Cook the fish, turning once, for 1–2 minutes, or until it is cooked and starts to blacken.

Cut a small wedge in the top of the muffins. Spoon in $1/2$ teaspoon of sour cream, then add a piece of fish and a coriander leaf. Serve hot.

Makes 24

turkish pizza

mini steak sandwiches

2 tablespoons olive oil
1 onion, thinly sliced
400 g (14 oz) fillet steak,
    about 1 cm (1/2 inch) thick
1 baguette, cut into 40 x 5 mm
    (1/4 inch) slices

salsa verde
1 large handful parsley
10 large basil leaves
20 mint leaves
1 garlic clove, crushed
1 tablespoon Dijon mustard
1 tablespoon capers
2 anchovy fillets
3 tablespoons olive oil

Heat the oil in a frying pan over low heat and cook the onion for about 25 minutes, or until caramelized.

To make the salsa verde, put the ingredients in a food processor and pulse to a thick paste. Season with salt and pepper.

Cut out 20 rounds from the steak with a 2.5 cm (1 inch) cutter. Season, then sear both sides on an oiled chargrill pan (griddle) for 1–2 minutes, or until cooked to your liking. Put a little of the onion on 20 rounds of bread, top with a piece of steak and a dollop of salsa verde, then sandwich with the remaining bread slices. Serve warm.

Makes 20

zucchini and haloumi fritters

2 large zucchini (courgettes)
4 spring onions (scallions),
   thinly sliced
200 g (7 oz) haloumi cheese,
   coarsely grated
30 g (1 oz/$\frac{1}{4}$ cup) plain
   (all-purpose) flour
2 eggs

1 tablespoon chopped dill,
   plus extra sprigs, to garnish
3 tablespoons oil
1 lemon, cut into 6 very thin
   slices, seeds removed
90 g (3$\frac{1}{4}$ oz/$\frac{1}{3}$ cup) thick
   plain yoghurt

Coarsely grate the zucchini and squeeze out as much liquid as possible in a clean tea towel. Combine the zucchini with the spring onion, haloumi, flour, eggs and chopped dill. Season well with salt and black pepper.

Heat the oil in a large heavy-based frying pan. Form heaped teaspoons of the mixture into fritters and cook in batches for 2 minutes on each side, or until golden and firm. Drain on crumpled paper towels.

Cut each slice of lemon into eighths to make small triangles.

Top each fritter with $\frac{1}{2}$ teaspoon of yoghurt, a piece of lemon and a small sprig of dill. Serve hot.

Makes about 45

coconut rice in banana leaves

2–3 young banana leaves, or foil
440 g (1 lb/2 cups) short-grain rice
185 ml (6 fl oz/3/4 cup) coconut milk

chicken filling
2 tablespoons oil
2–3 garlic cloves, crushed
6 curry leaves
1 teaspoon dried shrimp paste (blachan)
2 teaspoons ground coriander
2 teaspoons ground cumin
1/2 teaspoon ground turmeric
250 g (9 oz) minced (ground) chicken
3 tablespoons coconut milk
1 teaspoon lemon juice

Cut away the central ribs of the banana leaves. The leaves will split into large pieces — cut these into twelve 15 cm (6 inch) squares. Blanch in boiling water briefly to soften them, then spread them out on a tea towel and cover.

Wash the rice well, then drain and put in a large heavy-based saucepan with 440 ml (15$\frac{1}{2}$ fl oz/1$\frac{3}{4}$ cups) of water. Bring slowly to the boil, then reduce the heat to very low, cover tightly and cook for 15 minutes. Put the coconut milk and 125 ml (4 fl oz/$\frac{1}{2}$ cup) of water in a saucepan and heat without boiling. Stir through the rice with a fork, then leave to cool.

To make the filling, heat the oil in a large heavy-based frying pan over medium heat, add the garlic and curry leaves and stir for 1 minute. Add the shrimp paste, coriander, cumin and turmeric and cook for 1 minute. Add the chicken and cook, breaking up with a fork, for 3–4 minutes, or until the chicken changes colour. Stir in the coconut milk and cook over low heat for 5 minutes, or until absorbed. Remove the curry leaves. Add the lemon juice and salt and pepper, to taste. Cool.

353

Put 1 heaped tablespoon of rice in the centre of each piece of banana leaf or foil and flatten to a 4 cm (1$\frac{1}{2}$ inch) square. Top with a heaped teaspoon of filling. Roll into a parcel and put, seam-side-down, in a steamer lined with banana leaf scraps. Steam, in batches, for 15 minutes. Serve at room temperature with chopsticks or small forks.

Makes 12

coconut rice in banana leaves

artichoke frittata

30 g (1 oz) butter
2 small leeks, sliced
1 garlic clove, sliced
6 eggs

110 g (3³/4 oz/¹/2 cup) bottled
    marinated artichoke hearts,
    drained and sliced
1 teaspoon chopped tarragon
lemon juice, to serve

Heat the butter in a 20 cm (8 inch) non-stick frying pan, add the leek and garlic and cook for 3–4 minutes, or until softened. Spread evenly over the base of the pan.

Lightly beat the eggs and season with salt and black pepper. Pour the eggs into the pan and arrange the artichoke slices on top. Sprinkle with the tarragon and cook over low heat for about 10 minutes, or until set, shaking the pan occasionally to evenly distribute the egg.

Put under a hot grill (broiler) for 3–4 minutes, or until just set and lightly golden. Cut the frittata into wedges and drizzle with a little lemon juice.

Makes 8 wedges

smoked cod frittata

500 g (1 lb 2 oz) smoked cod
250 ml (9 fl oz/1 cup) milk
8 eggs
65 g (2¼ oz/⅔ cup) grated
   Parmesan cheese
60 g (2¼ oz/½ cup) grated
   Cheddar cheese

2 tablespoons chopped thyme
1 large handful basil, torn
2 tablespoons olive oil

Put the smoked cod in a saucepan with the milk and enough water to cover. Bring to the boil, then reduce the heat and simmer for about 3–4 minutes. Remove the cod with a slotted spoon and flake the flesh.

Whisk the eggs in a bowl and add the cheeses, thyme, basil and the fish. Mix together well.

Heat the oil in a 23–25 cm (9–10 inch) heavy-based frying pan. Pour in the mixture and cook over medium heat for 10 minutes, or until set. Put under a hot grill (broiler) for 3–4 minutes, or until just set and lightly golden. Cut into wedges for serving.

Makes 12 wedges

Using lemon grass stems as skewers allows their fragrance to permeate the chicken and makes a handle for dipping.

chicken and lemon grass skewers

5 stems lemon grass
1 kg (2 lb 4 oz) chicken thigh fillets,
    cut into 2 cm (3/4 inch) cubes
9 French shallots (eschalots), cut in half
3 tablespoons soy sauce
3 tablespoons mirin
2 tablespoons sugar
1 stem lemon grass (white part only),
    extra, finely sliced
1 red chilli, seeded and finely chopped

Trim the leaves off the lemon grass stems. Cut the thicker ends of the stems into 10 cm (4 inch) lengths, then into quarters lengthways. Make a small slit in the centre of each chicken cube and through the shallot pieces, to make threading easier.

Thread alternate pieces of chicken and shallot onto the lemon grass stems, using two pieces of chicken and one piece of shallot for each stem.

Mix together the soy sauce, mirin and sugar.

Cook the skewers in a hot chargrill pan (griddle) or frying pan for about 3–5 minutes. Brush the skewers with half the soy mixture as they cook, turning frequently. Add the sliced lemon grass and chilli to the remaining soy mixture and serve with the skewers, for dipping.

Makes 18

chicken and lemon grass skewers

seared scallops with lime

16 scallops on the shell
1 tablespoon vegetable oil
1/4–1/2 teaspoon sesame oil
1 tablespoon chopped chives

toasted sesame seeds, to garnish
1–2 limes, cut into 16 small
   wedges

Preheat the oven to 180°C (350°F/Gas 4). Using a sharp knife, carefully cut the scallops from their shells, as cleanly as possible, and remove the vein and white muscle. Wash the shells in hot water and warm through on a baking tray in the oven for 5 minutes.

Mix together the vegetable oil, sesame oil, chives and some salt and pepper, and toss the scallops in the mixture.

Sear the scallops in a hot frying pan for 30 seconds each side, or until just cooked through, being careful not to overcook. Return the scallops to the shells. Garnish with the sesame seeds and serve with the lime wedges.

Makes 16

crab and lime quiches

2 sheets ready-rolled puff pastry
2 eggs
185 ml (6 fl oz/3/4 cup) coconut
    cream
finely grated zest of 1 lime

2 teaspoons lime juice
200 g (7 oz) tinned or fresh
    crab meat, drained
1 tablespoon chopped chives

Preheat the oven to 210°C (415°F/Gas 6–7). Using two 12-hole round-based patty tins, lightly grease 18 of the holes. Cut 18 rounds from the puff pastry using an 8 cm (3¹/4 inch) cutter and put them into the holes.

Beat the eggs lightly in a small bowl and add the coconut cream, lime zest, lime juice, crab meat and chives. Season with salt and white pepper. Spoon 1 tablespoon of filling into each pastry case.

Bake for 20 minutes, or until golden. The quiches will rise during cooking, then deflate slightly. Serve warm.

Makes 18

Take care not to overcook the scallops; their flavour and texture are best when the centre resembles opaque glass.

scallops with goat's cheese and crispy prosciutto

16 scallops on the shell
4 thin slices of prosciutto
2–3 tablespoons extra virgin olive oil
1 tablespoon chopped flat-leaf (Italian) parsley
$^1/_2$ teaspoon sea salt flakes
100 g (3$^1/_2$ oz) goat's cheese, crumbled
2 tablespoons good-quality aged balsamic vinegar

Preheat the oven to 180°C (350°F/Gas 4). Using a sharp knife, cut the scallops from their shells, as cleanly as possible, and remove the vein and white muscle. Wash the shells in hot water and warm through on a baking tray in the oven for 5 minutes. Return the scallops to the shells.

Cook the prosciutto under a hot grill (broiler) until crisp, then drain on paper towels and break into small pieces.

Put the scallops on two baking trays. Combine the oil and parsley in a small bowl and season with sea salt and cracked black pepper. Brush the mixture over the scallops.

Cook the scallops in batches under a hot grill (broiler) for 2–3 minutes, or until they are tender.

Top the scallops with the goat's cheese, prosciutto and a drizzle of balsamic vinegar. Serve with small cocktail forks to avoid messy fingers.

Makes 16

seared scallops with lime and scallops
with goat's cheese and crispy prosciutto

pork dumplings

250 g (9 oz) minced (ground) pork
125 g (4 1/2 oz) raw prawn (shrimp) meat, finely chopped
60 g (2 1/4 oz/1/4 cup) bamboo shoots, chopped
3 spring onions (scallions), finely chopped
3 mushrooms, finely chopped

1 celery stick, finely chopped
1/2 capsicum (pepper), finely chopped
1 tablespoon dry sherry
1 tablespoon soy sauce
1 teaspoon sesame oil
1/2 teaspoon chopped seeded chilli
50 won ton wrappers
soy sauce, for dipping

Put the pork, prawn meat, bamboo shoots, spring onion, mushrooms, celery, capsicum, sherry, soy sauce, sesame oil and chilli in a bowl and mix together well.

Put a heaped teaspoon of filling in the centre of each won ton wrapper. Brush the edges with a little water, then gather the wrapper around the filling to form a pouch, slightly open at the top.

Steam in a bamboo or metal steamer over a saucepan of simmering water for 15 minutes, or until cooked through. Serve with soy sauce.

Makes 50

chicken dumplings

375 g (13 oz) minced (ground) chicken
90 g (3¼ oz) ham, finely chopped
4 spring onions (scallions), finely chopped
1 celery stick, finely chopped

3 tablespoons bamboo shoots, chopped
1 tablespoon soy sauce
1 garlic clove, crushed
1 teaspoon grated fresh ginger
50 won ton wrappers
soy sauce, extra, for dipping

Put the chicken, ham, spring onion, celery, bamboo shoots, soy sauce, garlic and ginger in a bowl and mix together well.

Put a heaped teaspoon of filling in the centre of each won ton wrapper. Brush the edges with a little water, then gather the wrapper around the filling to form a pouch, slightly open at the top.

Steam in a bamboo or metal steamer over a saucepan of simmering water for 15 minutes, or until cooked through. Serve with soy sauce.

Makes 50

Betel leaves have their own subtle yet unique taste that imparts an exceptional flavour to these fresh, minty parcels.

beef cha plu parcels

1 leek, trimmed
1 tablespoon oil
250 g (9 oz) minced (ground) lean beef
1 Lebanese (short) cucumber, finely chopped
1/2 red onion, finely chopped
6 Vietnamese mint leaves, finely chopped
2 tablespoons lime juice
2 tablespoons fish sauce
2 tablespoons desiccated coconut, toasted
45 large cha plu (betel leaves)
250 ml (9 fl oz/1 cup) sweet chilli sauce

Cut the leek in half lengthways, wash thoroughly and discard the outer layers and any hard core. Put the leek in a bowl, pour boiling water over it and soak for 5 minutes, or until softened. Drain well and set aside.

Heat the oil in a frying pan and cook the beef, breaking up any lumps with a wooden spoon, for 5–8 minutes, or until cooked through and browned. Remove from the heat and cool slightly.

Put the mince, cucumber, onion, mint, lime juice, fish sauce and coconut in a large bowl and mix together well.

Cut the base off the leek and cut it lengthways into thin strips about 5 mm (^{1}/4 inch) wide. Trim the betel leaves, then wash and dry well.

Put 1 teaspoon of the beef mixture in the centre of each leaf and roll the leaf up to form a cigar shape. Carefully tie with pieces of leek. Arrange on a platter and serve immediately with sweet chilli sauce.

Makes about 45

beef cha plu parcels

ratatouille mini pies

3 tablespoons olive oil
1 eggplant (aubergine), diced
1 onion, finely chopped
1 red capsicum (pepper), diced
1 zucchini (courgette), diced
1 tablespoon tomato paste
   (purée)

1 large tomato, chopped
1 teaspoon dried Italian herbs
750 g (1 lb 10 oz) ready-rolled
   shortcrust pastry
1 egg, lightly beaten
ready-made or home-made
   pesto, to serve

Heat 2 tablespoons of the oil in a frying pan and cook the eggplant until golden. Remove. Heat the remaining oil in the pan and cook the onion, capsicum and zucchini for 2 minutes. Stir in the tomato paste, tomato, herbs and eggplant. Cook for 20 minutes, or until reduced. Leave to cool.

Preheat the oven to 180°C (350°F/Gas 4) and put a baking tray in the oven. Lightly grease 24 mini muffin holes.

Roll the pastry thinly and cut out 24 rounds with a 7 cm (2³/4 inch) cutter. Repeat with a 5.5 cm (2¹/4 inch) cutter. Put a large round in each muffin hole and fill with the cooled filling. Dampen the edges of the small rounds and put them on top of the filling to seal the pies. Brush with egg. Put the tin on the hot baking tray and cook for 25 minutes, or until golden. Cool slightly, then remove from the tin. Serve with pesto.

Makes 24

cheese fondue

1 garlic clove, cut in half
3 tablespoons white wine
200 g (7 oz/1$\frac{1}{2}$ cups) grated
   Gruyère cheese
185 g (6$\frac{1}{2}$ oz/1$\frac{1}{2}$ cups) grated
   Cheddar cheese

small mushrooms, cauliflower
   and broccoli florets, and
   crusty bread, to serve

Rub the inside of a fondue dish with the garlic clove, add the white wine to the dish and bring to the boil. Reduce the heat to a simmer, add the Gruyère and Cheddar and stir until the cheeses melt completely. Cook over low heat for 4–5 minutes.

Serve with the mushrooms, cauliflower, broccoli and bread to dip in the fondue, using a skewer or a fork.

Serves 4

spring onion pancakes with chinese barbecue pork

spring onion pancakes
125 g (4^1/$_2$ oz/1 cup) plain (all-purpose) flour
2 teaspoons oil
1^1/$_2$ teaspoons sesame oil
2 spring onions (scallions), thinly sliced
oil, for pan-frying

1 tablespoon oil
175 g (6 oz) Chinese barbecue pork, cut into 24 slices
1 garlic clove, crushed
2 tablespoons hoisin sauce
1 teaspoon oyster sauce
1 teaspoon soy sauce
1 teaspoon sugar
^{1}/$_2$ teaspoon sesame oil
1 teaspoon cornflour (cornstarch) mixed with
    125 ml (4 fl oz/^{1}/$_2$ cup) cold water
coriander (cilantro) sprigs, to garnish

To make the pancakes, sift the flour and ^{1}/$_4$ teaspoon of salt into a bowl, make a well in the centre and add the oil and 100 ml (3^1/$_2$ fl oz) of boiling water. Stir well until the mixture is moistened and a soft dough forms.

Turn onto a floured board and knead for 5 minutes, or until the dough is smooth and elastic. Use more flour if necessary to prevent the dough sticking. Cover the dough with a tea towel and rest for 15 minutes.

Roll the dough into a long sausage shape, then cut into 24 pieces. Shape each piece into a ball, then flatten into a 5–6 cm (2–2^1/$_2$ inch) round. Brush each round with sesame oil and sprinkle with spring onion. Roll the pancakes like a Swiss roll, then flatten with your hands. Roll again from the other side, then shape into 4 cm (1^1/$_2$ inch) rounds. Stack the pancakes on baking paper and rest for 15 minutes.

Heat the oil in a wok and stir-fry the pork over high heat for 1 minute, then add the garlic and toss for 30 seconds. Add the sauces, sugar and sesame oil. Pour in the cornflour paste and stir until the sauce boils and thickens. Remove from the heat.

Pour 1 cm (^{1}/$_2$ inch) of oil into a frying pan and heat to 180°C (350°F), or until a cube of bread browns in 15 seconds. Cook the pancakes in batches for 1–2 minutes on each side, or until golden. Drain on paper towels.

To serve, put one slice of the pork topping onto each pancake and garnish with a sprig of coriander. Serve warm.

Makes 24

cheese fondue

burgundy beef mini pies

2 tablespoons olive oil
500 g (1 lb 2 oz) diced lean beef
1 onion, finely chopped
50 g (1³/4 oz) pancetta, finely
　chopped
2 garlic cloves, crushed
1 tablespoon tomato paste
　(purée)

250 ml (9 fl oz/1 cup) red wine
125 ml (4 fl oz/¹/2 cup) beef stock
1 teaspoon dried thyme
125 g (4¹/2 oz/¹/2 cup) puréed
　tomatoes
750 g (1 lb 10 oz) ready-rolled
　shortcrust pastry
1 egg, lightly beaten

Heat half the oil in a large saucepan over high heat and cook the beef
in batches for 5 minutes, or until browned. Remove. Add the remaining
oil and cook the onion, pancetta and garlic for 3–4 minutes, or until soft.
Return the meat to the pan, stir in the tomato paste, wine, stock, herbs
and tomato, then cover and simmer for 50–60 minutes, or until tender.
Cook, uncovered, for 30 minutes, or until the sauce has reduced. Cool.

Preheat the oven to 180°C (350°F/Gas 4) and put a baking tray in the oven.
Grease 24 mini muffin holes. Roll the pastry thinly and cut out 24 rounds
with a 7 cm (2³/4 inch) cutter. Repeat with a 5.5 cm (2¹/4 inch) cutter. Put
a large round in each muffin hole and fill with the cooled filling. Dampen
the edges of the small rounds and put them on top of the filling to seal
the pies. Brush with egg. Put the tin on the hot baking tray and cook for
25 minutes, or until golden. Cool slightly, then remove from the tin.

Makes 24

zucchini patties

2 zucchini (courgettes), grated
1 small onion, grated
30 g (1 oz/¼ cup) self-raising
    flour
35 g (1¼ oz/⅓ cup) grated
    kefalotyri or Parmesan
    cheese

1 tablespoon chopped mint
2 teaspoons chopped parsley
pinch of ground nutmeg
25 g (1 oz/¼ cup) dry
    breadcrumbs
1 egg
olive oil, for pan-frying

Put the zucchini and onion into the centre of a clean tea towel, twist as tightly as possible and squeeze dry. Combine the zucchini, onion, flour, cheese, mint, parsley, nutmeg, breadcrumbs and egg in a large bowl. Season well with salt and cracked black pepper, and mix with your hands to a stiff mixture that clumps together.

Heat some olive oil in a large frying pan over medium heat. Drop level tablespoons of the mixture into the pan and cook for 2–3 minutes, or until well browned all over, turning once. Drain well on paper towels and serve hot. The patties can be served plain sprinkled with salt or are delicious served with tzatziki (see page 122).

Makes 24

These colourful vegetable shapes are delicious slathered with zesty sour cream and topped with fried leek.

vegetable shapes with sour cream and fried leek

2 x 425 g (15 oz) long, thin orange sweet potatoes, peeled
5 beetroots
125 ml (4 fl oz/1/2 cup) sour cream
1 garlic clove, crushed
1/4 teaspoon finely grated lime zest
oil, for deep-frying
2 leeks, cut into long, thin strips

Put the sweet potatoes in one large saucepan of water and put the beetroots in another. Bring them to the boil over high heat and simmer, covered, for 30–40 minutes, or until tender, adding more boiling water if it starts to evaporate. Drain separately and set aside until cool enough to handle. Remove the skins from the beetroots and cut them lengthways into 1 cm (1/2 inch) slices. Cut the sweet potato into 1 cm (1/2 inch) rounds. Using a biscuit cutter, cut the slices and rounds into shapes. Leave to drain on paper towels.

Put the sour cream, garlic and lime zest in a bowl and mix together well. Refrigerate until ready to use.

Fill a deep heavy-based saucepan one-third full of oil and heat to 190°C (375°F), or until a cube of bread dropped in the oil browns in 10 seconds. Tie a few strips of leek into a knot and deep-fry for 10 seconds, or until lightly golden and crisp. Drain on crumpled paper towels and season with salt. Repeat with the remaining leek strips to make 35 knots in total.

To assemble, put a teaspoon of the sour cream mixture on top of each vegetable shape and top with a fried leek knot.

Makes about 35

Vegetable shapes with
sour cream and fried leek

crunchy thai chicken and peanut cakes

3 teaspoons grated palm sugar
   or soft brown sugar
1 tablespoon fish sauce
350 g (12 oz) minced (ground)
   chicken
120 g (4^{1}/$_{2}$ oz/^{3}/$_{4}$ cup) toasted
   peanuts, chopped
40 g (1^{1}/$_{2}$ oz/^{1}/$_{2}$ cup) fresh
   breadcrumbs
1 tablespoon Thai red curry
   paste

1 tablespoon lime juice
3 makrut (kaffir lime) leaves,
   very finely shredded
2 tablespoons sweet chilli sauce
2 tablespoons chopped
   coriander (cilantro) leaves
125 ml (4 fl oz/^{1}/$_{2}$ cup) oil
1 banana leaf, cut into 24 x
   5 cm (2 inch) square pieces
sweet chilli sauce, extra,
   to serve

Dissolve the sugar in the fish sauce, then put in a bowl with the chicken, peanuts, breadcrumbs, curry paste, lime juice, lime leaves, sweet chilli sauce and coriander. Mix well. Divide the mixture into 24 small balls — they will be quite soft. Flatten into rounds about 1.5 cm (^{5}/$_{8}$ inch) thick. Lay them in a single layer on a tray, cover and refrigerate for 30 minutes.

Heat the oil in a heavy-based frying pan and cook the cakes in batches for 2–3 minutes on each side, or until firm and golden. Drain on paper towels.

Put a chicken cake on each square of banana leaf and top with a dash of sweet chilli sauce. Secure with a toothpick for easier serving.

Makes 24

bagna cauda

400 ml (14 fl oz) cream
1–2 tablespoons olive oil
6 anchovy fillets
1 garlic clove, crushed

assorted crudités, such as celery
    sticks, scrubbed baby carrots,
    baby beans and radishes,
    spring onions and quartered
    baby fennel, to serve

Bring the cream to the boil in a small saucepan, then reduce the heat and simmer for 15 minutes, or until the cream has thickened and reduced by about half.

Heat the oil in a small frying pan over medium heat and cook the anchovy fillets and garlic for 1–2 minutes, stirring to break up the anchovy. Add this to the cream and whisk over low heat for 1 minute.

Spoon into a serving bowl and serve with crudités to dip in the hot sauce.

Serves 6

Light, crispy and bursting with flavour, the won ton wrappers seal in the scallop juices and their dressing in one mouthful.

scallop pockets

24 large scallops
1 tablespoon oil
5 cm (2 inch) piece fresh
    ginger, grated
4 spring onions (scallions),
    finely chopped
1 tablespoon Chinese rice
    wine or dry sherry

2 teaspoons sesame oil
1 teaspoon cornflour
    (cornstarch)
24 won ton or egg noodle
    wrappers
oil, for pan-frying
24 blanched garlic chives

Using a sharp knife, remove the vein and white muscle from the scallops. Leave any roe attached.

Heat the oil in a frying pan, add the ginger and spring onion and cook over medium heat for 2 minutes, stirring occasionally. Increase the heat and, when the pan is very hot, add the scallops and stir-fry, tossing quickly, for 30 seconds. Remove the pan from the heat.

Blend the rice wine, sesame oil, cornflour and a little salt and pepper in a small bowl until the mixture forms a smooth paste. Pour over the scallops, return to the heat and toss over high heat for 30 seconds, or until the liquid has thickened. Cool completely.

Working with one won ton wrapper at a time and keeping the rest covered, brush the edges lightly with water. Put a scallop in the centre, bring up the sides and pinch together to form a pouch with a frill at the top. Transfer to a lined baking tray and cover with a clean tea towel. Repeat with the remaining wrappers and filling.

Heat 2 cm (3/4 inch) of oil in a frying pan to 180°C (350°F), or until a cube of bread dropped in the oil browns in 15 seconds. Add the scallop pockets in batches and cook for 5 minutes, or until golden brown. Drain well on crumpled paper towels. Tie a blanched garlic chive around each one and serve immediately.

Makes 24

bagna cauda

baguette with egg, dill pesto and prosciutto

8 thin slices of prosciutto
1 French bread stick, sliced
  diagonally into 30 pieces
45 g (1^1/$_2$ oz/1 heaped cup)
  chopped dill
80 g (2^3/$_4$ oz/^{1}/$_2$ cup) pine nuts,
  toasted
2 garlic cloves, crushed

65 g (2^1/$_4$ oz/^{2}/$_3$ cup) finely
  grated Parmesan cheese
4 tablespoons virgin olive oil
10 g (^{1}/$_4$ oz) butter
7 eggs, lightly beaten
4 tablespoons milk
1 tablespoon light sour cream

Preheat the oven to 200°C (400°F/Gas 6). Put the prosciutto on a baking tray lined with baking paper. Bake for 5 minutes, or until sizzling and crisp. Put the bread on baking trays and bake until golden on both sides.

Put the dill, pine nuts, garlic and Parmesan in a food processor and finely chop. With the motor running, add the oil in a thin stream and process until smooth. Season. Spread the dill pesto over the bread slices.

Heat the butter in a non-stick frying pan over low heat. Add the combined eggs and milk. As the egg begins to set, use a wooden spoon to scrape the base to bring the cooked egg to the surface. Continue for 10 minutes, or until cooked but still creamy. Remove from the heat and stir in the sour cream. Season. Spread the egg on the toasts and top with torn prosciutto.

Makes 30

paprika lamb

18 French-trimmed lamb cutlets
1 tablespoon olive oil
1/4 teaspoon ground cumin
1/2 teaspoon smoked paprika

1 garlic clove, crushed
lemon wedges, to serve

Put the lamb cutlets in a large bowl with the olive oil, cumin, paprika, garlic and a pinch of salt. Mix well, then cover and refrigerate for at least 3 hours, preferably overnight.

Preheat an oiled barbecue hotplate or chargrill pan (griddle) to high and cook the cutlets for 4–6 minutes, turning once. Season with black pepper and serve with the lemon wedges to squeeze over.

Makes 18

Mildly spicy and deeply musky, paprika brings both flavour and colour to the dressing for these meltingly tender kebabs.

spanish-style beef kebabs

1 kg (2 lb 4 oz) rump steak, trimmed and cut into 2 cm (3/4 inch) pieces
3 garlic cloves, chopped
1 tablespoon chopped flat-leaf (Italian) parsley
4 tablespoons lemon juice
1/2 teaspoon black pepper
lemon wedges, to serve

paprika dressing
2 teaspoons paprika
large pinch of cayenne pepper
2 tablespoons red wine vinegar
4 tablespoons olive oil

Put the steak, garlic, parsley, lemon juice and pepper in a bowl, mix well, then cover with plastic wrap and marinate in the refrigerator for 2 hours. Meanwhile, soak 20 small wooden skewers in water for about 1 hour to ensure they don't burn during cooking.

To make the paprika dressing, whisk the paprika, cayenne pepper, vinegar, oil and $1/2$ teaspoon of salt together until well blended.

Preheat an oiled barbecue hotplate or chargrill pan (griddle) to high. Thread the pieces of marinated steak onto the skewers. Cook the kebabs, turning occasionally, for 4–5 minutes, or until cooked through. Drizzle with the paprika dressing and serve hot with lemon wedges.

Makes 20

paprika lamb

phad thai

100 g (3½ oz) 5 mm (¼ inch) thick dried rice noodles
1 tablespoon vegetable oil
1 egg, lightly beaten
2 teaspoons small dried shrimp
2 teaspoons sugar
2 teaspoons tamarind purée
1 tablespoon fish sauce

2 teaspoons lime juice
¼–½ teaspoon chilli powder
90 g (3¼ oz/1 cup) bean sprouts
2 teaspoons garlic chives, cut into 2 cm (¾ inch) lengths
40 g (1½ oz/¼ cup) dry-roasted peanuts, chopped

Soak the rice noodles in boiling water for 8 minutes, then drain. Heat the oil in a wok over medium heat and cook the egg until firm. Remove from the wok and slice thinly.

Add the dried shrimp and noodles to the wok and stir-fry over high heat for 1 minute, or until the noodles begin to turn golden. Add the sugar, tamarind, fish sauce, lime juice and chilli powder and stir-fry for 1 minute. Stir in the bean sprouts, garlic chives and egg slices, and cook until the bean sprouts wilt.

Spoon into eight small bowls or noodle boxes, sprinkle the peanuts over the top and serve with chopsticks.

Serves 8

chicken san choy bau

1 1/2 tablespoons vegetable oil
1/4 teaspoon sesame oil
3 garlic cloves, crushed
3 teaspoons grated fresh ginger
6 spring onions (scallions),
    thinly sliced
500 g (1 lb 2 oz) minced
    (ground) chicken
115 g (4 oz/2/3 cup) drained
    water chestnuts, finely
    chopped

90 g (3 1/4 oz/1/3 cup) drained
    bamboo shoots, finely
    chopped
3 tablespoons oyster sauce
2 teaspoons soy sauce
3 tablespoons sherry
1 teaspoon sugar
4 small witlof (chicory/Belgian
    endive) heads, leaves
    separated
oyster sauce, extra, to serve

Heat the oils in a wok or large frying pan, add the garlic, ginger and half the spring onion and stir-fry over high heat for 1 minute. Add the chicken and cook for 3–4 minutes, or until just cooked, breaking up any lumps.

Add the water chestnuts, bamboo shoots, oyster and soy sauces, sherry, sugar and the remaining spring onion. Cook for 2–3 minutes, or until the liquid thickens a little. Cool slightly, then divide among the witlof leaves (you will need about 2 heaped teaspoons per leaf). Drizzle with oyster sauce and serve immediately.

Makes about 36

Mini pappadams are an elegant way to serve a delicious curry as a nibble when you're in the mood for something substantial.

lamb korma on mini pappadams

2 tablespoons korma curry paste
1 garlic clove, crushed
1 teaspoon ground coriander
125 g (4^1/$_2$ oz/^{1}/$_2$ cup) thick plain yoghurt
350 g (12 oz) lamb backstrap or loin fillet,
    cut into 1.5 cm (^{5}/$_8$ inch) cubes
oil, for deep-frying
24 mini (4 cm/1^1/$_2$ inch) pappadams or larger ones
    broken into 24 pieces (chilli flavour, if available)
1 tablespoon oil, extra
1^1/$_2$ tablespoons mango chutney
small coriander (cilantro) leaves, to garnish

Combine the curry paste, garlic, ground coriander and half the yoghurt in a non-metallic bowl and stir until well combined. Add the lamb and coat well. Cover and marinate in the refrigerator for 1–2 hours.

Fill a deep heavy-based saucepan one-third full of oil and heat to 180°C (350°F), or until a cube of bread dropped in the oil browns in 15 seconds. Cook the pappadams a few at a time for a few seconds each, or until they are puffed and lightly golden. Remove with a slotted spoon and drain on crumpled paper towels.

Heat a wok over high heat, add the extra oil and swirl to coat. Add the marinated lamb in batches and cook, stirring, for 4–5 minutes, or until the lamb is cooked through. Spoon a heaped teaspoon onto each pappadam and top with $1/2$ teaspoon of the remaining yoghurt, then $1/4$ teaspoon of chutney. Garnish with a coriander leaf and serve immediately.

Makes 24

phad thai

empanada

250 g (9 oz/1 cup) Italian
    tomato passata
1 tablespoon pickled jalapeño,
    chopped, plus 1 tablespoon
    of juice from the jar
2 tablespoons roughly chopped
    coriander (cilantro) leaves
1 teaspoon olive oil
1/2 red onion, finely chopped

1 garlic clove, crushed
150 g (51/2 oz) minced (ground)
    beef
1 teaspoon tomato paste (purée)
1/4 teaspoon ground cumin
1/8 teaspoon sweet paprika
3 sheets ready-rolled shortcrust
    pastry
1 egg yolk, beaten

Put the passata, pickled jalapeño and juice in a saucepan and cook over medium heat for 5 minutes. Allow to cool, then stir in the coriander.

Heat the oil in a frying pan over medium heat and cook the onion, garlic, beef, tomato paste, cumin and paprika for 3–4 minutes, stirring often to break up the meat. Remove from the heat, season and allow to cool.

Preheat the oven to 180°C (350°F/Gas 4). Using an 8 cm (31/4 inch) cutter, cut 16 rounds from the pastry. Put 1 tablespoon of the beef mixture in the centre of each round and brush around the edge with beaten egg yolk. Fold the pastry over to make a half-moon shape, and press the edges together firmly. Brush the tops with egg yolk and bake for 15–18 minutes. Serve warm with the spicy tomato sauce.

Makes 16

polenta wedges with bocconcini and tomato

1 tablespoon olive oil
250 g (9 oz/1^2/$_3$ cups) polenta
75 g (2^1/$_2$ oz/^{3}/$_4$ cup) grated
   Parmesan cheese
2^1/$_2$ tablespoons ready-made
   or home-made pesto

150 g (5^1/$_2$ oz) fresh bocconcini
   cheese, thinly sliced
12 cherry tomatoes, cut into
   quarters
1 handful basil, larger leaves
   torn

Grease a 20 x 30 cm (8 x 12 inch) baking tin with the olive oil. Bring 1 litre (35 fl oz/4 cups) of lightly salted water to the boil in a saucepan. Add the polenta in a steady stream, stirring continuously to stop lumps forming. Reduce the heat to very low. Simmer, stirring regularly, for 20–25 minutes, or until the polenta starts to come away from the sides of the pan. Stir in the Parmesan and season well. Spoon the polenta into the baking tray and smooth the top with the back of a wet spoon. Leave for 1 hour, or until set.

Once the polenta has set, carefully tip it out onto a board and cut it into 24 x 5 cm (2 inch) squares, then cut each square into two triangles. Chargrill the polenta in batches on a preheated chargrill pan (griddle) for 2–3 minutes on each side, or until warmed through.

Spread each triangle with 1 teaspoon of the pesto, and top with a slice of bocconcini and a tomato quarter. Season and grill (broil) for 1–2 minutes, or until the cheese just starts to melt. Garnish with basil and serve hot.

Makes 48

beef en croute with béarnaise sauce

500 g (1 lb 2 oz) piece beef eye fillet, trimmed
    and tied at even intervals with string
2 teaspoons oil
60 g (2 1/4 oz) butter, melted
1 garlic clove, crushed
2 small bread sticks, cut into 40 very thin slices
25 g (1 oz) mustard cress, cut into short lengths

béarnaise sauce

200 g (7 oz) butter, melted
4 tablespoons white wine vinegar
1 bay leaf
1 tablespoon chopped tarragon
6 black peppercorns
3 parsley sprigs
2 egg yolks
2 teaspoons chopped tarragon, extra

Preheat the oven to 180°C (350°F/Gas 4). Heat the oil in a frying pan. Season the beef, add to the pan and brown all over. Transfer to a small baking dish and bake for 20–25 minutes for medium to medium–rare.

Combine the butter and garlic in a bowl and brush over both sides of the bread. Bake on baking trays for 10 minutes, or until just golden.

To make the sauce, melt the butter slowly in a saucepan over low heat. Remove from the heat and leave for 2–3 minutes so the milky mixture separates to the bottom. Carefully pour off the butter, leaving the milky sediment behind; discard the sediment. Put the vinegar, bay leaf, tarragon, peppercorns and parsley in a saucepan and simmer briefly until reduced to 1 tablespoon. Strain. Beat the egg yolks and the reduced sauce in a heatproof bowl over a pan of simmering water until slightly thickened. Remove from the heat and drizzle in the butter a few drops at a time, beating continuously until thick. If the butter is added too quickly, the mixture will separate. Stir in the extra tarragon and season to taste. If the mixture is too thick (it should be the consistency of mayonnaise), stir in a little water.

Cut the beef into very thin slices, drape over each crouton and top with some sauce. Garnish with the mustard cress and serve.

Makes 40

empanada

calamari romana

350 g (12 oz) cleaned small
   squid tubes
1/2 teaspoon salt
40 g (1 1/2 oz/1/3 cup) plain
   (all-purpose) flour

1/4 teaspoon black pepper
oil, for deep-frying
lemon wedges, to serve

Cut the squid into 1 cm (1/2 inch) wide rings. Combine the squid rings with the salt, then cover and refrigerate for about 30 minutes. Dry on crumpled paper towels.

Combine the flour and black pepper in a bowl. Fill a deep heavy-based saucepan one-third full of oil and heat to 180°C (350°F), or until a cube of bread dropped in the oil browns in 15 seconds. Flour a few squid rings at a time and cook, turning with a long-handled spoon, for 3 minutes, or until lightly browned and crisp. Flour the remaining batches just before frying. Drain on paper towels and serve hot with the lemon wedges.

Makes about 30

tomato and haloumi skewers

48 basil leaves
250 g (9 oz) haloumi cheese,
    cut into 1.5 cm ($^5/_8$ inch)
    pieces
150 g ($5^1/_2$ oz) semi-dried
    (sun-blushed) tomatoes

2 tablespoons balsamic vinegar
2 tablespoons extra virgin
    olive oil
1 teaspoon sea salt

Soak 24 small wooden skewers for 1 hour to prevent burning. Thread a basil leaf onto a skewer, then a piece of haloumi, a semi-dried tomato, another piece of haloumi and another basil leaf. Make 24 skewers.

Put the skewers on a preheated barbecue hotplate or chargrill pan (griddle) and cook, turning occasionally, until the cheese is golden brown, brushing with the combined vinegar and oil during cooking. Sprinkle with sea salt and serve warm.

Makes 24

Iced water is the magic ingredient that makes tempura batter so light and crispy, and the finished dish so incredibly addictive.

mixed tempura

12 raw king prawns (shrimp)
1 sheet of nori, cut into 12 thin strips
250 g (9 oz/2 cups) tempura flour or
    plain (all-purpose) flour
500 ml (17 fl oz/2 cups) iced water
2 egg yolks, lightly beaten
oil, for deep-frying
flour, for coating
60 g (2 1/4 oz) broccoli florets
100 g (3 1/2 oz) button mushrooms
1 red capsicum (pepper), cut into thin strips
soy sauce, to serve

Peel and devein the prawns, leaving the tails intact. Cut a little slit in the underside of each prawn (this will prevent them curling) and wrap a piece of nori around the base of the tail.

Sift the flour into a bowl, make a well in the centre and add the iced water and egg yolk. Stir with chopsticks until just combined. The batter should be slightly lumpy.

Fill a deep heavy-based saucepan one-third full of oil and heat to 180°C (350°F), or until a cube of bread dropped in the oil browns in 15 seconds.

Dip the prawns in flour to coat, shake off any excess, then dip in the batter. Add the prawns to the oil in batches and cook until crisp and light golden. Drain on paper towels. Repeat with the broccoli, mushrooms and capsicum. Serve the tempura immediately with soy sauce for dipping.

Makes about 30

mixed tempura

gulab jamun

100 g (3$^{1}/_{2}$ oz/1 cup) powdered
   milk
50 g (1$^{3}/_{4}$ oz/$^{1}/_{3}$ cup) blanched
   almonds, ground
155 g (5$^{1}/_{2}$ oz/1$^{1}/_{4}$ cups) plain
   (all-purpose) flour
1 teaspoon baking powder

$^{1}/_{2}$ teaspoon ground cardamom
30 g (1 oz) butter, chopped
60 g (2$^{1}/_{4}$ oz/$^{1}/_{4}$ cup) plain
   yoghurt
220 g (8 oz/1 cup) sugar
a few drops of rose water
oil, for deep-frying

Sift the dry ingredients into a bowl. Rub in the butter with your fingertips until the mixture resembles fine breadcrumbs. Make a well, then add the yoghurt and 2–3 tablespoons of water. Mix with a flat-bladed knife to form a soft dough. Shape into small balls, then cover with a damp cloth.

Put the sugar and 375 ml (13 fl oz/1$^{1}/_{2}$ cups) of water in a saucepan and stir until the sugar dissolves. Simmer for 5 minutes. Stir in the rose water.

Fill a heavy-based saucepan one-third full of oil and heat to 180°C (350°F), or until a cube of bread browns in 15 seconds. Deep-fry the dough balls in batches until deep brown. Don't cook them too quickly or they won't cook through. They should puff up a little. Drain in a sieve set over a bowl. Put the warm balls in a deep bowl and pour the syrup over the top. Leave to soak and cool until still slightly warm. Drain and serve piled in a bowl.

Makes about 35

chocolate coffee cups

200 g (7 oz/1 1/3 cups) dark
   chocolate melts (buttons)
20 foil confectionery cups
1 tablespoon cream

50 g (1 3/4 oz/1/3 cup) chopped
   white chocolate
1 tablespoon coffee liqueur
20 chocolate coffee beans

Put the chocolate melts in a heatproof bowl. Bring a saucepan of water to the boil, remove from the heat and sit the bowl over the pan, making sure the bowl does not touch the water. Stir occasionally until the chocolate has melted. Cool slightly.

Working with one foil cup at a time, put 1 teaspoon of melted chocolate in each. Use a small paintbrush to coat the inside with chocolate, making sure it is thick and there are no gaps. Turn the cups upside down on a wire rack and leave until firm. Return the remaining chocolate to the bowl over steaming water for later use.

Combine the cream, white chocolate and coffee liqueur in a heatproof bowl. Stir over a saucepan of simmering water until smooth. Cool slightly, then spoon into the chocolate cups. Press a coffee bean into each cup. Allow to set. Re-melt the reserved chocolate. Spoon it over the filling and tap to level, then leave to set.

Makes 20

Lounge parties are the perfect place to indulge in a bit of retro chic — for that personal touch, add your own messages.

chinese fortune cookies

3 egg whites
60 g (2^1/4 oz/^{1}/2 cup) icing (confectioners') sugar, sifted
45 g (1^1/2 oz) butter, melted
60 g (2^1/4 oz/^{1}/2 cup) plain (all-purpose) flour

Put the egg whites in a bowl and whisk until just frothy. Add the icing sugar and butter and stir until smooth. Add the flour and mix until smooth. Set aside for 15 minutes.

Preheat the oven to 180°C (350°F/Gas 4). Line a baking tray with baking paper. Draw three 8 cm (3^1/4 inch) circles on the paper, then turn the baking paper over.

Using a flat-bladed knife, spread 1^1/$_2$ level teaspoons of the cookie mixture over each circle. Bake for 4–5 minutes, or until slightly brown around the edges.

Working quickly, remove the cookies from the baking trays by sliding a flat-bladed knife under each one. Put a folded written message inside each cookie.

Fold the cookies in half, then in half again over a blunt-edged object. Allow to cool on a wire rack and cook the remaining mixture in the same way. Make only three cookies at a time, otherwise they will harden too quickly and break when folding. If this happens, return the tray to the oven and warm them through.

Makes 20

chinese fortune cookies

rich chocolate truffles

185 ml (6 fl oz/3/4 cup) thick
    (double/heavy) cream
400 g (14 oz) good-quality
    dark chocolate, grated

70 g (2^1/2 oz) butter, chopped
2 tablespoons orange liqueur
dark cocoa powder, for coating

Put the cream in a small saucepan and bring to the boil. Remove from the heat and stir in the chocolate until it has completely melted. Add the butter and stir until melted. Stir in the orange liqueur. Transfer to a bowl, cover and refrigerate for several hours or overnight, or until the mixture is firm enough to roll.

Quickly roll 2 teaspoons of the mixture into balls, and refrigerate until firm. Roll the balls in the cocoa, shake off any excess and return to the refrigerator. Serve at room temperature.

Makes about 40

rum and raisin truffles

60 g (2^{1}/$_4$ oz/^{1}/$_2$ cup) raisins,
    finely chopped
3 tablespoons dark rum
200 g (7 oz) chocolate-coated
    wheatmeal (wholemeal)
    biscuits, crushed
60 g (2^{1}/$_4$ oz/^{1}/$_3$ cup) soft
    brown sugar
1 teaspoon ground cinnamon

50 g (1^{3}/$_4$ oz/^{1}/$_2$ cup) pecans,
    finely chopped
3 tablespoons cream
250 g (9 oz/1^{2}/$_3$ cups) chopped
    good-quality dark chocolate
90 g (3^{1}/$_4$ oz/^{1}/$_4$ cup) golden
    syrup
125 g (4^{1}/$_2$ oz/1 cup) pecans,
    extra, finely ground

Combine the raisins and rum in a small bowl and marinate for 1 hour. Put the crushed biscuits, sugar, cinnamon and chopped pecans in a large bowl and mix together well.

Put the cream, chocolate and golden syrup in a saucepan and stir over low heat until melted. Add to the biscuit mixture, stir in the rum and raisins and mix to combine. Refrigerate until the mixture is just firm enough to roll into balls.

Roll 2 teaspoons of the mixture into balls, then roll the balls in the ground pecans. Refrigerate until firm.

Makes about 60

Densely chewy yet delicate, these chocolate cups with a filling of caramel and cream will send your tastebuds into orbit.

chocolate caramel cups

150 g (5¹/₂ oz/1 cup) dark chocolate melts (buttons)
18 small foil confectionery cups
80 g (2³/₄ oz) chocolate fudge caramel bar, chopped
3 tablespoons cream
50 g (1³/₄ oz/¹/₃ cup) white chocolate melts (buttons)

Put the dark chocolate melts in a small heatproof bowl. Bring a small saucepan of water to the boil and remove from the heat. Sit the bowl over the pan, making sure the bowl does not touch the water. Stir occasionally until the chocolate has melted.

Using a small new paintbrush, brush a thin layer of chocolate inside the foil cases. Stand the cases upside down on a wire rack to set. Return the remaining chocolate to the bowl over steaming water for later use.

Combine the chopped fudge bar and cream in a small saucepan and stir over low heat until the fudge has melted and the mixture is smooth. Transfer to a bowl and leave until just starting to set, then spoon into each foil cup, leaving about 3 mm ($1/8$ inch) of space at the top.

Re-melt the reserved dark chocolate, spoon it into the caramel cases and tap to level. Leave to set.

When the dark chocolate has set, melt the white chocolate in the same way as the dark chocolate. Spoon it into a small paper piping bag and drizzle patterns over the cups, or just spoon a small amount on each. Leave to set.

Makes 18

index

432